HOPE
on the Broken Road

JUD WILHITE

WORTHY
PUBLISHING

Copyright © 2013 by Jud Wilhite

Published by Worthy Publishing, a division of Worthy Media, Inc., 134 Franklin Road, Suite 200, Brentwood, Tennessee 37027.

Worthy is a registered trademark of Worthy Media, Inc.

Library of Congress Control Number: 2013946676

All Scripture quotations, unless otherwise indicated, are taken from the Holy Bible, *New International Version*®, *NIV*®. Copyright © 1973, 1978, 1984 by Biblica, Inc.™ Used by permission of Zondervan. All rights reserved worldwide.

Scripture quotations marked NLT are taken from the Holy Bible, *New Living Translation,* copyright © 1996, 2004. Used by permission of Tyndale House Publishers, Inc., Wheaton, Illinois. All rights reserved. Scripture quotations marked MSG are taken from *The Message.* Copyright © 1993, 1994, 1995, 1996, 2000, 2001, 2002. Used by permission of NavPress Publishing Group. Scripture quotations marked NKJV are taken from the New King James Version. Copyright © 1982 by Thomas Nelson, Inc. Used by permission. All rights reserved.

Published in association with Yates & Yates, www.yates2.com.

This book is adapted from *Throw It Down* by Jud Wilhite.

ISBN: 978-1-61795-211-1 (hardcover)

Cover design: Susan Browne Design
Photo credit: Getty Images
Photographer: David Epperson
Interior design: Kimberly Sagmiller, FudgeCreative.com

Printed in China
13 14 15 16 17 18 HAHA 8 7 6 5 4 3 2 1

To members of the Central Christian Church recovery team who give so much to help others experience freedom.

Contents

INTRODUCTION

The Road Out

I wake deep in the night, heart pounding frenetically from a cock-tail of drugs, shivering in a cold sweat, my own saliva spilled in thick threads onto my face and chest. Barely able to rise and stand, I look in the mirror, and the morose images reflected there swim around my head: purple sores, hollow cheeks, lost weight, vacant eyes. Seventeen and going on ninety, I no longer care about the terrible risk of recapturing a high that increasingly eludes me.

Gathering myself, I line up my considerable stash and take it all. I surrender myself to the mercy of the drugs. For the longest time, coming in and out of consciousness, I find myself gripping the bumper of my old red Fiero, throwing up violently, finding a strange comfort in the fact I will soon be dead . . .

Later, I come to. Every part of my body hurts. As I wake, I feel the weight of a dark despair unhinging. The window blinds are pulled; I don't know what time of day—or even what day—it is. Lying on the floor too exhausted to move, I take in the soft and subdued light spilling around me. I am reminded somehow of grace. For the first time in my life, totally aware that I have hit rock bottom, I desire to be free.

This book is about that desire for freedom and how I, along with many others, have experienced rescue, redemption, and hope. It *is* possible for you to be free and embrace the life God has for you. It *is* possible to become the person you were meant to be, the person you long to be. It *is* possible to experience life change.

We all have something we'd like to be freed from, something that is holding us back. Maybe your issue is subtler than mine.

- Maybe you struggle with *perfectionism*.
- Perhaps you are *addicted to approval*.
- *Anger* could be wreaking havoc in your life.
- Your *manipulative ways* with people may have ruined every romantic relationship you've had.
- Maybe you *overwork, overeat, overdrink,* or *overshop* and have realized that you are being held captive by that behavior.

Whatever broken road you are walking, let my experience of drug addiction be a metaphor, a picture, of the very real challenges you face and the very real hope that is available to you. I understand—I have lived out—the reality that the very thing you desire, what you hope will set you free from the pain—whether that pain is rooted in shame, loneliness, grief, failure, rejection, or something else—actually enslaves you. The issues in each case are the same; only the specifics of the enslavement vary.

But wait a minute! As enslaved as you are, you nevertheless found the strength to open this book. That step reveals a loosening of the master's chains. Be encouraged that you have found this map for traveling the road out of bondage. Know that the truth you encounter on this road will set you free (John 8:32).

Seem too good to be true? Then, for right now, let me believe for you that the truth—that God's truth set forth in these pages—will, by his grace, set you free.

Jud Wilhite
Las Vegas, Nevada

1

Homecoming

In the days following my nearly fatal overdose, I realize my serious lack of real options. Exhausted by endless cycles of disappointment, hurt, suffering, and guilt, I come to understand at a very deep level my inability to save myself.

I can die, go crazy, or get help.

So I cry out.

A few weeks after my overdose, I drop to my knees in my bedroom and say the only prayer I can muster: "God, help me. I'm messed up beyond belief. I need you." As my words fade, I listen to the sound of the unbalanced ceiling fan squeaking above me. No voice speaks audibly to me. In my heart, though, two words slowly take shape in my consciousness: Welcome home.

Only when I admitted my powerlessness to God did my life begin to change. The Bible says, "The fear of the LORD is the beginning of wisdom, and knowledge of the Holy One is understanding" (Proverbs 9:10). That fear doesn't mean we walk around in terror. It means that we revere God and respect him. The foundational aspect of wisdom does not begin with a degree, but with faith in the character and nature of the God of the Bible.

A harmful habit is rarely the direct result of a thing we do; a harmful habit tends to arise because of an idol we create and worship.

Acting on the false hope of satisfying our deepest cravings for significance, comfort, security, meaning, approval, and, ultimately, love, we often place our trust in alternative saviors and swear allegiances to artificial gods. We seek to design our own agendas rather than trust in a God who asks that we give away our lives for the sake of others.

When we place our faith in such tiny gods, we sin, which literally means "to miss God's mark," and we inevitably find ourselves on a path to heartache. Think of all the broken relationships and torn lives left in the wake of greed, lust, gossip, and the relentless pursuit of success. Consider, too, all the years of life we human beings waste in self-destructive patterns and self-defeating behaviors.

Wasteland Exodus

During my four-year wasteland of addiction, my parents make me go to church. Promising to go to youth group, I walk through the church into nearby alleys and kill time smoking cigarettes. I observe people walking into the church building, but I don't really understand the attraction. When I reconnect with my parents, we play out the same conversation.

"What did you learn about in church, son?"

"Jesus," I say.

"And what about Jesus?"

"That he loves me."

I answer in this way because I believe this is what they wish to hear.

Secretly, deep in my brokenness, it is what I long to believe.

The biblical book of Exodus—that word literally means "the road out"—provides deep insights about moving out of captivity. Exodus chronicles the journey of the Israelite people from slavery to a new life of freedom in ways deeply applicable to our own individual and contemporary journeys.

From slavery, God led the people of Israel into freedom. In the ancient wisdom of the biblical narrative, the book of Exodus foreshadows the movement into the full life promised by Jesus.

The account begins and ends with God's redemption. Exodus explains the great lengths God went in order to accomplish the liberation of his people. He reveals himself to be both *with* and *for* his people.

By the power and grace of God, the Exodus account can bring us back to our true selves, destinies, and stories.

Even in the depth of a great desperation, we are not only reminded but also empowered to take the road out. And, like all great Old Testament stories, Exodus points to the reality of Jesus, who came to "heal the brokenhearted, to proclaim liberty to the captives" (Luke 4:18 NKJV).

With a self-sacrificing love, Jesus bore the divine punishment and curse of sin, setting us free by God's power and grace.

All roads out of whatever enslaves us eventually lead us to the love of Jesus, our heart's true home.

 Life or Death

My own road out of a deadly addiction eventually led me to the church. Only God in his mercy and irony could take a messed-up kid lost in addiction, piece him back together, get him through college and graduate school, and deploy him in the self-proclaimed City of Sin. In Las Vegas, there are no culture wars. Morality disappeared long ago. Today, built on a billion-dollar marketing machine, the city annually yields some of the highest rates in the nation for everything bad: drug use, domestic violence, addictions, and divorce.

And today, twenty-two years into my recovery, I pastor Central Christian Church, a church with campuses in unlikely Las Vegas locations and beyond. When tempted to despair over the long odds of this ministry, I trace the roots of my faith back to a day on the freeway, a few weeks after my nearly fatal overdose at the age of seventeen. Driving my red Fiero down a Texas interstate at seventy miles per hour, I found a supernatural power to throw my drugs out the window. In the days that followed, sweaty and clammy and grumpy, I understood the life-or-death nature of my circumstances and whispered my prayers continually: "I can't do this alone. God, help me. If you don't show up, I'm through."

He showed up.

Life Change

In time, God gave me the grace to return to church on my own terms. Surrounded by a handful of redeemed men and women, I experienced recovery in a community of people who walked with me, listened to me, and coached me off the edge. They were not scared away by my problems or doubts. God used the church to save my life. And then, through the church, he led me back into the pain of a broken world—and he can do the same for you, whatever the causes and whatever the symptoms of your brokenness.

I have seen Jesus work in my own life and in the lives of thousands of individuals in our church who now experience freedom. Drugs should have killed me, and they almost did. But God provided the road out, and a community of faith continues to sustain me. Together, we have come to understand the irony of a power springing from powerlessness, and we have found that an overwhelming dependence on God sets us and others free. God's grace moves in power and love, often incognito, for the redemption of people trapped in the bondage of sin and pain.

Together, we fight for freedom in the moment-by-moment reality of gratitude. We share what we have experienced and continue to experience through the Person and work of Jesus, who lived, died, and rose again for our freedom. His sacrifice on the cross provided that path to pardon, and his resurrection opened up to us a road of life. Without shame, we follow God in order to find and fulfill our true purpose—bringing him glory, serving him, delighting in the freedom he grants us, and helping others walk in it as well.

No matter what you have done or where you have been, no matter what is enslaving you, God in his love has made a road out from slavery to sin and self-defeating behaviors, a road to freedom. In the following pages, I'll share core principles that have freed thousands of people. I'll share the stories of several people to inspire your own journey, whatever the starting point of captivity is. Life change does happen. Your future can be different. Tomorrow does not have to repeat the mistakes of yesterday.

Turn Right

For years, across the street from our original church campus in the Las Vegas area, strobe lights would shoot into the night sky from an adult bookstore. Directions to the church were easy: follow the lights to the "Live Nude Adult Bookstore" and turn right to the church. I like that because it's such a stark picture of repentance. We are all only a turn away from freedom.

So what's holding you back? What's weighing you down? You can break free. I know this step can be scary, but I encourage you to see it as an opportunity. This is a chance for you to be free.

Just a Minute

List the top three things holding you back from freedom with God, yourself, and others.

2

Beautiful Shambles

If we are honest with ourselves, we know what is holding us back from living a life of freedom. If asked, we could identify the specific destructive patterns, emotions, identities, or histories that weigh us down. And, if we have wrestled long enough with these difficult realities, most of us would also admit to a growing awareness of our powerlessness to do anything about them. That admission is a good thing—*if* we let our powerlessness move us past defeat and prompt us to look up to God for help.

Whenever Lance contemplates his plan for recovery, the same images always play through his head . . .[1]

In his mind's eye, he first sees himself playing golf with his father, as he has twice a week for eighteen years, and then he startles with the phone's ring and bristles with the news of his dad's heart attack . . .

Then Lance finds himself with his wife, on the morning of their ninth anniversary, standing in front of the television, watching the slow and surreal implosion of the World Trade Center Towers from the force of two Boeing 767s—one of which he recognizes as a plane he had previously piloted . . .

Then his mind shifts to eighteen months later when, spirit deflated, he hands in his wings after an aviation career that spanned thirty-five years.

Lance shakes his head to clear the images. He reminds himself of all the reasons they called him "Captain"—the discipline he inherited from his military father, the perseverance he learned from his polio-stricken mother, and the skill he used to become a much respected pilot. And, at fifty-eight, Lance believes the newly discovered holes in his life can be fixed. He must simply form the right plan.

Despite being faced with the loss of his identity and a hint of his own mortality, Lance feels no overwhelming need for God. One reason is that Lance continues to invest in the concept of control. Plus, he harbors anger with God over his father's death and his mother's wheelchair. So, turn to God? No. Close friends? No, he never really allowed for any. Family? No, they didn't really share feelings like these.

So, Lance logically concludes, why not a drink? It once worked to put him at ease in social situations, and who could argue with the occasional college kegger or the Friday night happy hour in the Officers' Club? He reasons that alcohol will take the razor's edge off of his life, so he can fully develop and then execute his own plan for redemption.

Help Wanted

Our habits often start innocently enough. Maybe you love to shop or enjoy eating great food. These are gifts from God. But if you allow these desires to run out of control, driven by a need to feel security or worth or love, you head straight for trouble.

Shopping is fine—until you have fifty thousand dollars (and counting) on your credit cards. Food is wonderful—until the doctor recommends a diet, yet your soul is so starved that you find yourself eating more and more.

Most of the idols we crave are good things we allow to control us. Sleep, food, sex, pleasure, and work are all God-designed realities for our good, but taken to extremes, these good things can yield laziness, obesity, lust, excess, and imbalance. Although we may not immediately recognize the dysfunction driving our behavior, we take the first steps on the road to freedom by naming destructive behaviors, acknowledging our slavery to them, and recognizing that we can't find healing alone. In other words, we need to honestly face the problem.

Sometimes God allows you to be placed in a position where there is nowhere left to turn but to him. In the middle of a struggle, it's tough to admit that you can't handle it by yourself and that you need help moving forward. Yet one of the greatest and most liberating moments in life occurs when you stop, reach out to God, and say the words, "I can't do this on my own." *Then* you are in a position to receive God's care and give him the glory for his work. An early church leader named Augustine put it like this: "God gives where he finds empty hands."

When you need help, recognize your need. Then ask God for help in getting that need met in a healthy way. Don't pretend you're in a position to help yourself. Perhaps God has allowed you to be in that position so you will turn to him and acknowledge your need.

In the grip of a consuming addiction, Lance invests the next few years in deceit—attempting to fill the void in his life with a secret supply of alcohol. He hides bottles in every room of his house, the back of toilets, the trunk of his car, his golf bag, even in a gas grill. Lance retreats into isolation, passionately fueling the void, abandoning any pretense of a social life or meaningful relationships. In the darkness of his depression, Lance seldom sees the light of day. And, free from the random drug testing, he continues to up the ante on his wager that alcohol will help the pain and fill the void.

In response to his wife's plea to get help, Lance calmly tells her he will after his first arrest—and, on that same day, he finds himself sitting in a less-than-five-star room at the El Segundo jail for a DUI. In the middle of the night, he awakes from a nightmare and reminds himself to pick up a fifth of Scotch from the liquor store upon his release.

The next day Lance suffers seizures in a hotel lobby and, if not for the persistence of a security officer, believes his dead body would have been found later in his room. Lance spends the next two weeks—including four days with ankles and wrists strapped to a bed—convulsing in an ICU unit, in and out of consciousness, suffering from a combination of withdrawal, pneumonia, liver abnormalities, severe depression, and water on the brain.

Finally, Lance has hit bottom. He knows it is "change or die" time. He sees that his carefully controlled world is in total shambles. For the first time ever, he admits he is powerless and cries out to God for help.

The Character of God

There are a lot of images of God out there in our culture. There's God as Morgan Freeman in *Bruce Almighty:* superb posture, great narrative voice, really stylish dresser. There's God as an animated Victorian-era cartoon in *Monty Python and the Holy Grail:* scary voice, no-nonsense attitude, hinged jaw, big crown, and robe. There's God as Ralph Richardson in *Time Bandits*: conservative business suit, a well-groomed grandfather running out of energy.

Your view of God affects virtually everything in your life. In the book of Exodus, the character of God unfolds as the story develops. In the opening chapters, Israel cries out and God responds with compassion. He pays attention to the pain of his people. Exodus tells us that "God *heard* their groaning and he *remembered* his covenant with Abraham, with Isaac and with Jacob. So God *looked on* the Israelites and *was concerned* about them" (Exodus 2:24–25, emphasis mine).

In response to the suffering of his people, God talks about his future work of redemption in terms of a love relationship.

- *He hears you.* Realize that the God of the universe actually hears your cry for help! He is not deaf to your need. Your prayers reach him, and he listens.
- *He remembers you.* God remembers why he created you, he remembers his relationship with you, and he remembers that by redeeming you, he is bringing glory to himself.
- *He looks on you.* God is watching you but not from a distance. He is watching you up close and personally. He is intimately involved in the details of your life.
- *He is concerned about you.* The word translated *concern* is used in a variety of ways, referring to simple perception and, at the other extreme, to a more intimate and relational knowledge. The point here is that God has a longstanding relationship with his people. From the depths of his being, God's mercy and

his intention to save flow like a mighty river. God is not idle; he is the Sustainer of life and the Author of history. He is concerned about you, and he will save.

Having once been addressed as "Captain," Lance knows that the process of surrender will be an ongoing one. He enters into a rehab program, has some positive results, and focuses on putting his faith and trust in Jesus. He gets intentional about his spiritual journey and finds a community of faith to help him grow.

Lance knows the road out will be a long one, and the journey starts with admitting that he can't do it on his own. His life has grown totally unmanageable. He starts to meet weekly with a recovery group, and he constantly asks God for help. He knows there is no way to freedom without the day-by-day, hour-by-hour help of God. Lance doesn't allow himself to get paralyzed with thoughts of tomorrow or next year; he focuses on trusting God and living free today. Slowly, painfully, Lance takes steps to freedom.

After a year of sobriety, Lance decides to make a public statement of his faith in Jesus, in the One who empowers and sustains his healing. Before his baptism, Lance looks out over the church and sees the people he loves surrounding him. It is his wife, once again, who stands beside him, also declaring her faith in Jesus. Together, they share the understanding of a supernatural and gracious God working in power and love for them. Lance reflects on his former life of isolation as he looks out on the sea of smiling faces, of new friends who helped in his rescue and of family members with whom he is now enjoying restored relationships. Once hidden and alienated from people, once lost in self-deception and secrets, Lance now finds great joy in sharing this moment with others.

Having once been addressed as "Captain," Lance must revisit again and again the reality of powerlessness. In contrast to his old self-assurance, Lance now understands that his life change will come only as he continues to completely and wholly depend on God. As Lance comes to grips with his new freedom—orchestrated only by the power and grace of God—he feels no need to control his own life and gladly surrenders, with increasing joy, to serving others.

"The first step of recovery is surrender," Lance says, "and my entire life had been based on being in control. I may never fully understand the circumstances and events that led to my nearly killing myself with alcohol, but I do now understand that I had a disease for which there is no cure. It may have been lying

dormant in my body like a cancer for many years, and when it appeared, there was no way I could control it. It's easier to surrender when you have no real choices."

Today Lance and his delightful wife give most of their free time to helping others experience recovery at Central Christian Church. As I've come to know Lance, the reality that always strikes me first is his smile—not just from ear to ear, but rising up from a soul, once broken and restless, now healed and at peace. Lance isn't perfect, but he knows the One who is—the One who continues to not only restore his people but also to magnify his life in them.

When you are most aware of your absolute powerlessness, God reveals his character, his love for you, and his power to transform you. Whatever you're up against in life, think about what it means that God hears you, remembers you, looks on you, and is concerned about you. He not only cares about your next breath, but he cares about your entire journey through life into eternity.

So admit that you can't—on your own—fully let go of your unhealthy ways or completely move on from the pain of poor decisions, other people's actions, or broken relationships.

Sure, you may be incredibly talented, strong, dynamic, and successful, but if you want to be free—well, that is another matter. Freedom comes only when you reach out to God, admit that you are powerless, and ask for his help.

Like the enslaved Israel, cry out to God in prayer. Throughout the Bible, you see short 9-1-1 prayers for help. Psalm 109:26 is one example: "Help me, oh help me, GOD, my God, save me through your wonderful love" (MSG). The next time you stand in line to buy a new thing with money you don't have, or scan the freezer for another ice cream sandwich you shouldn't eat, or consider gossiping about a cousin you don't like, or contemplate a business deal that would compromise your character, whisper a short prayer: "Help me! Help me, God, my God! Save me through your wonderful love."

And then walk—or, better, run—away from that temptation or thought.

The Bible says, "Through Christ Jesus the law of the Spirit of life set me free from the law of sin and death" (Romans 8:2). When we surrender to Jesus, God's Spirit comes to dwell inside of us. When he does, we have the power to yield to the law of the spirit of life rather than to the law of sin and death.

So ask God's Spirit to help you face the challenges in your life. Depend on the Spirit and trust him to pull you through. He can set you free from sin and death!

Just a Minute

Which aspect of God do you find most encouraging today? Why?

He hears you.

He remembers you.

He looks on you.

He is concerned about you.

3

Throw It Down

Admitting that we need the help of a God who desires our freedom establishes for us the possibility of change. When we surrender to God, we move out of his way so that the change he wants for us—and, ideally, that we've come to want—can happen.

But what does it mean to surrender to God? For years, I wrongly believed in a God who mostly desired my boredom. If I surrendered to God, I believed I would end up losing who I am. I could see myself in a shirt with a pocket protector and plaid pants, looking like a junior accountant. What I didn't understand was that, because he created me, God knows what makes me tick and that when I surrendered to God, he would take me to places that would optimize the design he'd built into me. There is nothing cheesy or boring about surrendering to God!

In *The Return of the King*, such a personal transformation

is evident in Aragorn, the king whose return has been foretold. Having spent several years dodging the reality that he is heir to the throne, he has roamed Middle Earth as Strider the ranger, a sort of cross between mercenary, bounty hunter, and border patrol agent. When Elrond, the king of the elves, hands the restored Sword of the West to Aragorn, Elrond tells Aragorn, "It is time to put away the ranger and become that which you were created to be." This is what happens in surrender: we begin to discover the person God created us to be, the person we desire in our heart of hearts to become.

What You Call "Home"

After throwing down a fifth of mescal tequila with her friend, Ashley warms to the possibilities of Las Vegas that awaken at midnight. Swallowing the worm from the bottom of the bottle, Ashley, a graduate of the University of Washington with a degree in political science, understands the cost. Having lost fifteen jobs in the five years since graduating, she's drawn to the city's high-wire pursuit of ecstasy and escape. She longs to find the road out of herself or, at the very least, the pain that increasingly defines her.

When Ashley howls at the moon, her friend suggests another bar, which leads to another bar, which leads to a closing drink at Shifty's Lounge, a biker's club. The sunrise ends another chapter in Ashley's story of weed, meth, small-time dealing, alcohol, Harleys, gambling, and eluding the law, of her surrender to the rush and blur of the Las Vegas lifestyle.

On the way home, Ashley's girlfriend passes out behind the wheel of the Firebird she is driving at seventy miles per hour. Hitting the median, the car flips, and Ashley, unbuckled inside, rolls over twice before her face spiders the windshield and several ribs crack along the dashboard. Then Ashley is thrown out the passenger-side window.

Coming to consciousness on the side of the road, pooled in her own blood from gaping head-to-toe wounds, Ashley does not feel overwhelming pain or trauma. Instead, she surrenders to a mysteriously strong sense of having been thrown down by a band of angels.

Years earlier, when she was sixteen, Ashley's life first spun out of control. She remembers hanging up the phone in her family's suburban home in Thousand Oaks, California, a mostly *blue-sky life being played out between Malibu and Hollywood. That day, as the knot in her stomach tightened, she wondered how she would explain to her mother the news from the naval officer—the report of her brother's psychotic break with reality. Ashley already felt as if it didn't matter if she went left or right; her mother could never be pleased. She couldn't help but think what new abuse this circumstance might ignite.*

But Ashley's greater fear was the possibility of losing her brother. Due to the general absence of their father, a prestigious pilot who had women in other cities, and the emotional distance of their mother, the two of them counted on each other for survival. All the early family photos show them together, and even now she considers Sean her best friend. They formed a team against long odds.

When Ashley told her mother a short time later that her son had been transferred to a mental ward for observation, Ashley's mother collapsed onto a kitchen bench, eyes glazing over as a permanent vacancy settled in.

Throughout the next several years, a variety of diagnoses—manic-depressive, schizophrenic, schizo-effective—were shoveled on Sean, and Ashley watched her brother slowly deteriorate into a shadow of his vibrant and sweet-souled self. With each of Sean's stays in a series of institutions, psychiatric wards, jails, hospitals, halfway houses, VA facilities, and the streets, Ashley had to deal not only with that huge loss but also with the accusations of her mother, who increasingly blames Ashley for not providing her the love, care, and support she deems necessary.

So Ashley retreats into her newfound loves of alcohol, weed, and her boyfriend while at the same time exhausting herself trying, to the best of her intoxicated ability, to both care for her brother and please a demanding mother who will never be pleased. Ashley fears not so much falling into a cycle of abuse, but learning to call it home.

Following her near-fatal accident—and years of addiction to numb both her physical pain as well as her feelings of failure—a friend suggests that God was trying to get her attention, and Ashley senses an inconsistency between who she has become and who she was created to be. Ashley begins to attend church, participate in rehab, and cut back on her party lifestyle.

More than eighteen months later, smoking a bowl of marijuana at her father's house, she realizes the distance between her efforts to heal and the still-painful reality of her life. In a moment of heart-wrenching clarity, she stands, goes into the bathroom, and sees her reflection in the mirror: with her bloated red face and angry countenance, she is a total loser, a person headed nowhere. She's thirty and alone, living with her father, smoking weed that she purchased after pilfering his wallet.

She packs another bowl, kneels again by the fireplace so the smoke can go up the chimney, and feels the familiar stab of pain in her knee, the most enduring reminder of her near-fatal accident. Rising with the smoke is Ashley's prayer of surrender. For the first time in her life, she understands how much her freedom depends on the power and love of God.

Two days later, after another friend tells her she can't do it alone, Ashley returns to her father's home, drinks the remaining beer in his refrigerator, and makes an appointment to attend her first AA meeting.

Excuses, Excuses

When Moses first met God in a burning bush and received the divine calling to lead Israel to freedom, he responded with logical doubts about the assignment. Who was he—a Hebrew shepherd wandering in a wasteland of exile—to confront the most powerful person on the planet? And suppose Pharaoh didn't know the name of Moses' God? And what if Pharaoh didn't listen to his outrageous demand to set the Israelites free?

Speaking from his limited and broken human nature, Moses stood in good company. Reluctance and the failure to surrender immediately to God's plan mark the life of many of God's leaders in the Old Testament. Gideon felt insignificant. Samuel feared that God's mission for his life would trouble a relationship with his friend and mentor. Isaiah believed he was too dirty and tainted. Jeremiah reasoned he was too young and uneducated. Targeting the heart of each person's doubts, God did his loving transformational work. Gideon became a mighty warrior, and Samuel, Isaiah, and Jeremiah, some of God's greatest prophets.

Similarly, your excuses may stand in the way of God's design and purpose for your life. Do you hold on to bitterness against someone who has abused you or refuses to change? Do you turn to a destructive habit—maybe nonstop work or constant gossip—to help you feel better about yourself? Do you believe you can prevent an addiction or negative habit from spinning out of control? Are you walking around in pain—from a divorce or a death—and building strong walls to keep out more pain?

Laying down a crippling emotion or habit is an act of surrender. You must move from thinking of God as out there somewhere to trusting him to know what heals you and then to lead you on the road to freedom. You must see your excuses for what they are: lame attempts to avoid the deeper issues that are blocking the healing God desires to accomplish in your life.

What's in Your Hand?

Thirteen years into sobriety, Ashley receives word of a good friend, also years into recovery, who hangs herself in despair after falling back into addiction. Ashley knows the power of her disease. She knows based on her own experience that even being thrown out the passenger-side window of a speeding car is not necessarily enough to bring one to a point of surrender.

At the same time, against long odds, Ashley finds hope: she has learned to listen to the whispers of God: "I continually ask God what he wants me to do. And then I listen. That doesn't mean I always follow what he wants me to do. But a degree of surrendering occurs when I listen to his suggestions. He is a gentleman and does not force me to do anything, but I've learned when I do it my way, it usually hurts a lot worse. Sometimes I ask him in anger, 'What do you want from me?' He waits for me to calm down and then whispers to me some more."

As a result of her own real-life experience and the community recovery programs she is involved in, Ashley feels privileged to offer that same hope to others, even if it might be only a whisper: *"I know where you are at, and it is not at all beyond the rescuing love and power of God."*

In the process of ongoing surrender, Ashley finds strength and peace and, yes, freedom in her new identity as a loved child of God: *"My Higher Power is Jesus, and he is around 24/7 to help me anytime I need it. He is my reason for living, and after all these years, we are still strong. He is my best friend. He never leaves me nor forsakes me. He is always with me."*

In the presence of God, Moses quickly learned the value of surrendering as he led the people of Israel on the journey from captivity to freedom. After listening to Moses' series of excuses, God decided to give him a visual lesson on the power of surrender. They engaged in the following conversation:

The Lord: "What's that in your hand?"

Moses: "A staff."

The Lord: "Throw it on the ground."

I believe the staff represents Moses' identity—his career as a shepherd and the source of his income. When God asked Moses to throw it down, God was calling for an act of surrender.

God was saying, "Release that thing you are holding onto that represents your career and your income, your life and your core identity. Throw it down before me."

When Moses did as God commanded, the staff became a snake and the leader-to-be ran away in fear. God told Moses to pick up the snake, and when he did, it became a piece of wood once again. The transformation mirrored the transformation Moses would go through—from shepherd to shepherd-leader.

That staff once used for sheep now signified Moses' new occupation: the shepherd and leader of God's people. After Moses picked up the staff, it was called "God's rod" and Moses was "God's person." By the love and power of God, Moses would be well suited for his new identity.

"What Is in Your Hand?"

What happened to Moses happens to us today when we surrender. When we lay down our lives, incomes, careers, hobbies, and habits before God—when we, in other words, die to
ourselves—we find new life in the process. We are to take up
our life again after God has blessed it, and we are to live for
him. As we do so—and whatever our brokenness was—we
experience the power of the new life of wholeness and hope.
This is part of what Jesus means when he says that to lose
your life is to find it (Matthew 10:39).

Moses began experiencing the life-transforming power of
the God who liberated him, who freed him to live according
to the divine design. All God required of Moses was surrender—the ongoing willingness to throw down his doubts, lim-
itations, destructive tendencies, and deeply residing fears.

God asks the same question of us: "What is in your hand?"
What are you holding onto that is keeping you from following the One who created you?

Only when you surrender yourself and take up the life
God designed for you will you experience the full extent of

God's healing work. Only then will you fully live the life he designed for you, the one you also desire in the deepest part of yourself.

Just a Minute

What are you holding onto that defines and/or protects you? Be specific. Will you throw down—or even just lay down— the very things you are clutching most tightly? Why or why not? What pressures or issues keep you from moving from the despair of powerlessness to the risk of surrender?

4

No More Games

A year after Bill's initial surrender to God, he is tackling a pen-and-paper inventory of his life. It has taken him years to begin and weeks to complete. Over time, his mother's stubborn tendencies to fight for him—her years of prayers, challenges, and steady forgiveness—have led him to living clean from meth, but what he sees in front of him now takes his breath away. A horrific number of pages record the hurt and damage caused by his life of destructive habits, resentments, and fears. Bill seizes on the idea of a tornado to communicate the kind of rubble he has left in his wake.

Gauging by the intensity of the pain that comes with reading those pages, Bill can see why he put off the fourth and fifth steps of recovery—honesty with yourself and honesty with God and others. The truths Bill has unearthed hurt like hell. At the same time, he understands in his gut that the healing process hurts and that his lack of honesty has him stuck. Bill continues *to engage in the lust of pornography, for example, but he rationalizes that as long as he's clean, does it really matter?*

Even deeper, at the places God has been at work in him, Bill realizes that his soul is not well. The painful process of taking this personal inventory shuffled the rocks in the dark places of his past, and there is no way of knowing what kind of creature may emerge. Desperately hoping that God will continue to work miraculously for him and in him, Bill gathers the pages that describe his past life and sets out to, one by one by one, make amends for all the wrongs he has done.

And somewhere along the way, Bill realizes that he feels himself running toward, and no longer away from, love.

Brutal honesty fuels our ongoing freedom. At the important intersections of the road out—at those points when we can choose to ditch denial, embrace dependence, and surrender to God—honesty plays an integral role. Yet honesty can be so difficult. We human beings have an amazing ability to shade the truth to our own advantage. We justify. We rationalize. And when it comes to our destructive issues, we have a tendency to outright lie to ourselves. We play games. We fool ourselves by thinking, *Tomorrow I'll get help. Tomorrow I'll start being honest with myself. Tomorrow I'll start working on getting better.* As we look toward an elusive future, we are immobilized by our self-destructive past. Honesty requires the commitment to live well in the present.

Taking Inventory

In my own experience, I built the bridge that moved me from tomorrow to today when I took a detailed personal inventory of my life, when I asked myself hard questions.

And you may be a lot like me. Do you have a difficult time admitting your weaknesses? Do you even like yourself? What have you done and said that hurt other people, and what have you done about those hurts you inflicted? What is different—or what do you want to be different—about the specific ways you follow up your hurtful words and actions today? How much does fear—of failure, of rejection, of success, of whatever—drive your life? What do you do to attempt to hide or protect yourself? What actions or habits do you rely on to establish emotional distance? God desires love, not fear, to steer your life.

The Exodus story reveals two opposing strategies for life. Pharaoh abused his power and coerced people for his own selfish gain. God used his power to liberate people. The book of Exodus contrasts the slavery of fear with the freedom to love.

And God calls us to love. He calls us to risk the honesty necessary to find freedom from fear's life-draining grip. When we get honest with ourselves, we must also be ready to get honest with God and others. This honesty builds momentum for our journey on the road to freedom. Coming clean with God and with other people releases a healing power in our lives. But this process starts only when we willingly take the risks inherent in letting out—and fully facing—the inner demons that drive our external behaviors.

The sheer amount of bottled-up stuff in our lives is shocking—and that reality became all too apparent several years ago when we launched a website that provided people with a safe place to be completely honest. We challenged people to simply dump their junk. They could anonymously write anything—yes, anything—they wanted. There were no rules, and I've never read anything quite so vulnerable and raw. People poured out their hearts online. They wrote without any filter, with no conventional layer of politeness, and with no religious faking it. The honesty with which they wrote was both frighteningly brutal and pure. We heard cries for help voiced as questions, yearnings, and confessions.

- *"I am addicted to the image of perfection at ALL times, even if it hurts those around me."*
- *"I turn to alcohol so I can feel NUMB—and all I really want is to feel LOVED."*
- *"I hate. I hate. I hate."*
- *"I was molested by my dad from the age of thirteen to the age of sixteen. I never told anyone, not even my mom, and now it's tearing me apart."*
- *"I feel lost and abandoned by God."*

These kinds of hurts and confessions stand in stark contrast to the interactions of people in most churches. On Sunday mornings we're tempted to play the game, to put on a show. As a pastor, I see it all the time: people are wrestling with depression they don't understand; anger that is on the verge of being out of control; failure to forgive a parent or spouse; sexual abuse suffered as a child; adultery, an abortion; a fresh mark of self-injury on the arm; a pink slip; money problems. Too often people say nothing about what is really going down, and often they are facing it alone—or not facing it at all.

Instead, we human beings spend our energy maintaining appearances rather than dealing with the deeper internal issues that drive our external behaviors. As a result, our spiritual growth ceases, and we find ourselves stuck in a holding pattern. Progress requires the ongoing confession of the brokenness that comes with living as a sinner in a world filled with sin.

In our contemporary culture, however, honesty often falls victim to "spin control." With the moral failings of celebrities like Tiger Woods, Jesse James, and John Edwards, the general concern is usually "What can this person do to restore his or her image?" The larger question—"Can his or her *character* be restored?"—is seldom addressed.

God does not want to improve our image; he wants to redeem and rebuild our lives. And what does God require of us in this process of transformation? Our honest admission of our sin and our honest recognition of the damage it does are key. Only then can we move forward in faith that we might be able to love others better.

Honesty requires a full confession: it's black or white; gray doesn't count. As we see in Bill's story, incomplete repentance is the temptation inherent in the act of confession. By failing to deal with the issue of pornography, Bill sacrificed the opportunity to move more honestly through life. He further cemented the connection between his addictive behaviors and the root issue of his fear of intimacy. When Bill chose honest confession, however, he learned to seek out the real, which is love, rather than the substitute—lust. Honesty opens the door to God's healing grace.

I find it tragic when we waste the opportunities God gives us to bring all of our life into his light. James 5:16 challenges us in the right direction: "Confess your sins to each other and pray for each other so that you may be healed." We are to pray for each other, but notice the condition for healing: *confession*. We'd rather camouflage our sins than confess them. Ideally, there should be at least one person in your life (your husband or wife, a pastor, or a friend) with whom you can share everything, someone you know will love and accept you unconditionally. Ultimately, the result of this confession is healing.

Showdown

The story of Exodus sets up a showdown. In one corner is Pharaoh, the king of a far-reaching empire who will stop at nothing to retain his power. In the opposite corner, you have the mysterious, virtually unknown God of a people enslaved by Pharaoh. With each new encounter with Pharaoh, God progressively revealed himself in all his sovereignty.

The significance of the plagues unfolds in God's showdown with Pharaoh, who is the self-proclaimed incarnate god of the sun, Ra. The plagues, presented in natural order, provided a dramatic platform for the showdown. The first two plagues—blood and frogs—were matched by the pharaoh's magicians, only to reveal that God was just getting warmed up.

Eugene Peterson wrote of God's progressive revelation of his power and sovereignty:

By the third, the mosquito plague, the magicians were clearly out of their depth, no longer able to match Moses blow for blow. After the sixth, the boils plague, the magicians were not only bested, they were incapacitated, put out of action by the boils. We hear no more of them. The four final plagues, anchored by the death plague, settle the sovereignty issue decisively. Pharaoh is skunked.[1]

But Pharaoh never found the courage to be honest with himself. Instead, as is the tendency of all dishonest men, he preferred to postpone surrender until tomorrow. Pharaoh had the opportunity to end his people's suffering. He simply had to let the Israelites go. Moses even gave Pharaoh the choice of when to do so. Pharaoh responded with: "Tomorrow. I'll let them go tomorrow."

Following the seventh and eighth plagues, Pharaoh articulated his remorse. Speaking to Moses, Pharaoh said, "Now forgive my sin once more and pray to the LORD your God to take this deadly plague away from me" (Exodus 10:17). His remorse, however, was short-lived. As the plague faded, Pharaoh changed his mind and refused to let Israel go. At the core of the problem lay Pharaoh's dishonesty. Despite his crumbling kingdom, Pharaoh could not release his power and—in behavior that becomes increasingly comic-tragic—refused to release the Israelites. He had multiple chances to change his life. Pharaoh's problem was that he didn't *really* want a changed life. All he wanted was a different situation.

It's the same with us. Our confession means nothing if it does not come from a heart desiring God and his good and perfect will for our lives. And the best clue to the true condition of our hearts is how often we put off a necessary surrender until tomorrow.

What Lies Beneath

The process of taking a personal inventory uncovers what lies beneath our denial and dishonesty.

As Bill reads through his detailed lists of ways he has hurt others, his mind settles on one moment when he was deep into his addiction to methamphetamines. Having moved back home, his life collapsing around him, he found a letter in his mother's jewelry box. Seeing his name in the salutation, he began to read: his mother was pleading for him to get help while informing him of the chaos he had created within the family, including her near divorce. Bill remembers the stab of pain he felt as he read those words, but, even worse, he remembers moving on from that pain when he found the perfect ring to pawn for his next high.

"There was a point where I put pen to paper and laid everything out—the good, the bad, and the ugly. I had to deal with my destructive habits, resentments, fears of living sober, and the pain and hurt I had caused my family and others. When I saw everything on paper, I couldn't deny it anymore: I really didn't understand how powerless I was until I saw everything on paper."

Stop *deceiving* yourself and you will stop *defeating* yourself. I learned this truth when I found myself wrestling with anger. Throughout my life anger has been an issue for me. Before I became a believer, it was a serious character flaw. I'd blow up in unpredictable ways at unexpected times. After surrendering to God, though, I began to deal with my anger, and I made some good strides. But ten years later anger reappeared in my life in significant ways: I was too harsh with loved ones, too controlled by my agenda.

When sins we thought we'd conquered or at least learned

to curb reemerge in our life, the tendency to play games is huge. Rather than deal with my anger, I told myself it was no big deal. I put it off and blew it off. After all, I was a Christian now and way better than I used to be, right? So I kept playing games, and the people closest to me paid the price. Then came the day when I found myself standing in the laundry room of our house staring at a hole I had just punched in the wall. It was a massive wake-up call. I had to stop deceiving myself and reach out to God and others for help with my anger.

When I took a personal inventory and an honest look at myself, I learned that a lot of my anger came from my being overcommitted.

I was traveling all the time and constantly stretched too thin at work. The result was constant stress: I felt like a Coke bottle shaken up and ready to explode at any moment. I had overcommitted to the point that if *anything* went wrong—a small delay due to car trouble, an extra errand my wife, Lori, needed me to run, a brief traffic jam on the freeway—it seemed that *everything* was wrong. Failing to take into account that life is full of delays and detours, I had concocted a recipe for disaster.

Often, we choose to play games because it's easier than tackling the difficult work of changing. I had to go back and completely reorganize my life. I made some hard decisions, and I stopped doing a lot of things that I didn't really need to be doing. I still struggle with a tendency toward anger, but I've learned new skills for how to handle it. And so can you if you are willing to get honest with yourself and look beneath the surface.

- Are you a perfectionist? Are things ever good enough for you?
- Do you bury yourself under unrealistic expectations you can't meet and then try to find release in a relationship or a substance or whatever?
- What about selfishness? Do you ever think about anyone else's needs and concerns, or are you completely consumed with what you want?
- Are you impatient?
- Are you dishonest?

These are hard questions, but answering them is crucial to leaving the broken road.

Just a Minute

Spend some time alone and write in your journal your answers to the questions above. As you answer honestly, don't despair. Jesus brings great hope. Confess, turn to Jesus, and experience God's power in your life.

Grace Spilling Over

I don't get it, but if you're into *The Price Is Right*, you're just into it. *The Price Is Right* has its own sort of cult following—and that cult includes my wife.

Lori comes by her affection for the show genetically, from her great-aunt Betty Sue. The two of them went to the show before Bob Barker retired. They had shirts made that said, "All roads lead to Bob's *The Price Is Right*!" (And they actually *wore* them!)

They got second-row seats for the show and, sure enough, Betty Sue heard those magic words, "Come on down! You're our next contestant on *The Price Is Right*!" Believe me, Betty Sue made all those years of faithful viewing pay off. She guessed the right price of a riding lawnmower and won it. Then she played the Flip-Flop Game (if you don't watch the show, I can't explain it) and won a vacation to Malaysia.

I confess: at this point in the show, I was almost as

excited as Lori was. I thought, *Way to go, Betty Sue! Please remember that we're related and that a riding lawnmower right now would be like getting underwear at Christmas. Malaysia, however, would be nice.*

Then, if that weren't enough, Betty Sue won the Big Wheel after a spin-off and made it all the way to the Showcase Showdown, where she finally lost. Still, for Betty Sue, the price was right more often than not.

The Bible speaks of the greatest price of all: the price Jesus paid to cover the cost of sin. The cost of sin is always so much greater than we anticipate. Yet even as the Scriptures tell us of the exorbitant price, they tell us it has already been paid by Christ's sacrificial death on the cross. Receiving God's grace and forgiveness is one of the most important steps we take on the road to freedom.

For many of us, forgiveness of another comes more easily than forgiving ourselves. Having survived abuse from others and our own destructive responses, our sense of self can feel so broken that shame becomes our identity, something for us to hide behind. As one person confessed to me, "I don't feel like I deserve good things. I can never deserve God's grace, and evidently I am not smart enough to stop trying to earn it."

But here's the really good news about grace: on the road to freedom, God never stops demonstrating his unlimited power and desire to redeem us.

Radical Risk

On the morning of a surgery that could take her father's life, Katie is there, by the side of the man who sexually abused her.

By entering her father's home, she ends an estrangement of years, a step necessary for her own continued healing. As she reads her Bible on the morning of the surgery, Katie is reminded of how deeply God's grace continually rescues and restores her, and she remembers that her forgiveness of her father will empower the healing process.

The proof: she is here.

"Here" in the sense of being away from someplace and also near. Away from the string of sexually and emotionally abusive father figures; away from the person she used to be, who obsessively weighed her self-esteem by the number of pounds consumed in the passion of her eating disorder; and away from the girl who was determined never to take another step in the name of love.

And near . . . to her father and her Father.

Katie knows the risk. Even after forgiving her father, she sometimes hears in her mind an inflection of his voice, the way he used to compliment her body, and she can't shake the feeling of danger.

As she sits in her father's house and reads through the Gospels, she sees Jesus—the One who pursues each of us in love and whose offer of grace startles her once again. From the rubble of her own broken soul, marriage, relationships, and life, Katie learns to understand that hurt people hurt people, and she experiences the role forgiveness plays in the supernatural process of her own healing.

After years of shame connected to her abuse and of even feeling responsible for that abuse, Katie accepts in the deepest part of her heart the gift of God's grace. She internalizes the fact that what happened was not her fault. She allows God's amazing mercy to heal her false perceptions of herself and her father.

She is here in her earthly father's house because of the heavenly Father: she is to extend to her father the kind of grace she has received from her Lord. She is here because of the places Jesus went for her—the cross and hell—so she could be free to face the obstacles blocking her own path, even if it means returning to the place where she experienced a hell of suffering.

While Katie is reading through the book of John on the morning of her father's surgery, he stumbles from his bedroom and asks what she is reading.

Freedom's Price

Exodus powerfully illustrates the price of gaining freedom from sin, shame, and brokenness. As God unleashed his power through a series of supernatural miracles directed against Pharaoh, Israel stood on the cusp of freedom. With each consecutive plague, God moved closer to introducing himself as the real ruler.

In the ninth plague, God defeated Pharaoh, the self-proclaimed incarnate god of the sun, by spreading darkness over the land. Pharaoh's reputation suffered irreparable damage. With the next plague, God went after Pharaoh himself by taking out his heir.

But this final plague signifies something deeper: Israel's recreation and rebirth as a free people and a free nation. In Exodus 12:21–23 we read:

Go at once and select the animals for your families and slaughter the Passover lamb. Take a bunch of hyssop, dip it into the blood in the basin and put some of the blood on the top and on both sides of the doorframe. Not one of you shall go out the door of his house until morning. When the LORD goes through the land to strike down the Egyptians, he will see the blood on the top and sides of the doorframe and will pass over that doorway, and he will not permit the destroyer to enter your houses and strike you down.

This passage describes what has come to be known as the Passover: God passed over every Israelite door that had blood on the doorframe and spared the life of the firstborn. The Passover marked the lives of the Israelites forever and is memorialized in a holiday.

Yet the liberation of God's people did not come without a cost. The price was the blood of a lamb and, as we see in Exodus 12, its outpouring was remembered in the context of a feast that celebrates God's miraculous work in the lives of his people.

Israel and You

Similarly, the New Testament teaches about a great price—paid for in the Person and work of Jesus Christ—and celebrated in the context of a great feast. The spilling of the blood of the "Lamb of God" (John 1:29) is remembered in the feast of the bread and wine of communion. At the end of history, the feast will culminate in the greatest celebration of all: the wedding supper of the Lamb. God's grace always calls for celebration.

Parallels between Israel and the church began with a great movement of God for freeing his people. But when Jesus willingly shed his blood, he rescued us from something more dreadful than slavery to a despotic king. Jesus rescued us from the slavery of sin that ultimately ends in death.

At the same time that God accomplishes our salvation, our obedience and our faithfulness are vitally important. If, for instance, the Israelites had not spread the blood of the Passover lamb on the doorframes of their houses, they would have died. God looked for blood on the door as a mark of obedience.

It's an odd place of limbo to navigate, but I have been

there myself: believing that God's grace exists for everyone but me. Many believers, no matter what they do, still can't shake the sense that past sins and mistakes condemn them. This inability to accept God's forgiveness drove me to the performance treadmill, where I tried harder and harder to earn the love of God. And failing despite my best efforts left me plenty of room to wallow in pointless guilt.

Henri Nouwen believed the greatest temptation in life resides not in success, popularity, or fame, but in self-rejection. When a person believes the negative and condemning voices that speak in the context of criticism or loneliness, he or she falls victim to the lie of condemnation and chooses to skip the recurring feasts of grace.[1]

Can you relate? In my own life, I considered my refusal of grace as somehow righteous, an acknowledgment of my deep brokenness. Only as God revealed to me that my refusal was a cancerous form of self-pity and pride was I able to see the deeper reality: by refusing grace, I was saying that Jesus was not enough and that his sacrifice needed to be greater. I was hearing the death rattle of pride: I was approaching the point where I could accept God's free gift of grace in the context of celebration and obedience. This process was initiated by God's salvation, but it was also something I became obedient to.

Guilt and Shame

Our obedience may also be needed if we're dealing with unhealthy guilt and shame. A vital difference exists between healthy and unhealthy guilt. Healthy guilt motivates us to amend relationships, make things right, and move toward health. It is focused more on others—on the impact of our wrong behavior on other people—than on ourselves. Unhealthy guilt, however, often results in self-hatred. We condemn ourselves. We refuse to believe we can ever be accepted.

Such shame debilitates. When I meet someone who wrestles with unhealthy guilt and forgiveness, I counsel that person to read Psalm 51, David's prayer for God's forgiveness after he committed the sins of adultery, murder, and lying. I challenge these hurting people to read Psalm 51 and ask for forgiveness for the specific sin that is still weighing them down. Then I tell them, "Don't ever ask God to forgive you for that sin again." Similarly, people who wrestle with shame find themselves thinking about their same sins over and over again. I share what the Bible says: "He has removed our sins as far from us as the east is from the west" (Psalm 103:12 NLT). God has removed our sins as far away from us as possible.

Confession of sin, of course, is a healthy and necessary biblical practice. However, constant confession of the same sin nourishes unbelief and inhibits genuine confession, often leaving the person paralyzed on the road out to freedom.

If you are that person, if unhealthy guilt weighs you down, read Romans 8 every day for the next two weeks. Really let the truths penetrate your heart. I believe that if you do so, you will experience God's forgiveness anew: "There is no condemnation for those who belong to Christ Jesus. And because you belong to him, the power of the life-giving Spirit has freed you from the power of sin that leads to death" (Romans 8:1–2 NLT).

This is the message of the good news: no condemnation! This message is for all who believe. So take heart and be encouraged. Grace is available to you solely because of who God is. Jesus sacrificed his life so that God could be both just in punishing sin and full of grace to you.

Grace on Grace

Katie smiles at her unshaven father, suspecting that his question is nothing more than the kind of small talk they have practiced for a lifetime—chatting about the weather or the pets or the character in a movie, a camouflage for truths that he deeply buries.

But how could Katie be casual when asked about the gospel? In her own healing journey, she has come to understand sharing the gospel as grace spilling over from one heart that is embracing the grace of God to another heart. Yet in the shadow of her father, she hesitates to answer.

Her father asks again, "What are you reading?"

When she blurts out, "The Bible," she expects a quick change of topic to maybe the chance of thunderstorms, but he asks, "What are you reading about?"

"Jesus" is what she tells him. And then, based on her own life experiences, she speaks of the grace Jesus offers, grace that frees her to deal with her own issues at the same time that it releases her to take new steps toward others in love. She explains to her

father how she is healing.

A few minutes later, kneeling with her father in his prayer to receive Jesus, Katie sees the tears of a broken man realizing that he is fully loved by his heavenly Father. In this moment, she learns that no matter how great the offense or how awful the abuse, healing depends on coming to grips with the reality of God's forgiveness.

Grace spills over from Katie's life into her father's life. The Spirit softens his heart and, in spite of his terrible mistakes and sin, provides him with a new beginning through repentance. For both father and daughter, shame disappears at the foot of the cross.

Just a Minute

What sin, if any, do you find yourself confessing again and again? Reflect on why doing so is neither necessary nor spiritually healthy. Also, practice sharing briefly and directly what God's grace has meant to you so that when the opportunity next arises, you—like Katie—can share this truth that sets us free.

Hope on the Broken Road

Freedom is a process that begins when we admit we are powerless over our struggle and we need help. We look up to God, believing that he listens, cares, and provides. We surrender to his will and get honest with him and with ourselves about our past and our mistakes. We depend on God's Spirit to give us strength. His grace is available to us and the price has been paid for our forgiveness, so we are able to live in and celebrate each moment.

And then comes catastrophe. The road out is not a fast lane, and the journey to freedom is stalled by potholes, dirt-road detours, and dead ends. Finding hope along a broken road requires a persevering faith.

In the heat of a Texas afternoon, Jennifer stands on the porch of her childhood home, wondering why she came. Her friends had warned her, "Don't go back," but she has hoped against hope that her relationship with her mom might somehow be repaired. After eighteen months of experiencing the supernatural power behind her sobriety, Jennifer reasons that at least some small chance of reconciliation exists.

Trembling, she walks into an empty living room, and the color of the carpet ignites a vivid flashback to her fifteenth birthday. As the images unwind, she sees herself standing in front of her mother, who is dressed for church and explaining once again to Jennifer why she can't go to church even if it is her birthday and Easter Sunday: "God hates you because you are evil . . ."

The words trail off as Jennifer runs out of the living room only to return with a prescription bottle of Motrin and 130 diet pills. In the slow motion of her recollection, Jennifer watches as she downs both bottles in front of her mom. And the last words she hears are her sister's, pleading with their mom to call an ambulance.

Now, as she waits for her mother, the memories continue to flood her mind. She sees herself on the living room sofa, sixteen years old, ninety-one pounds, and almost always three sheets to the wind . . . She sees herself hooked on a concoction of ecstasy, acid, cocaine, and marijuana, and purging most of her meals, lying in a New Orleans hotel room on a morning after Mardi Gras. Hers is the face of an eighteen-year-old on a three-week *binge, awakening to the realization she has used the last of the drugs, even the ones she was supposed to deal . . .*

Jennifer hears a noise and considers running out of the house and grabbing the first bus back to California, the residence of her recovery. But at just that moment, her mother interrupts the thought. As Jennifer makes her way into the living room, her mother announces that the basement bar is fully stocked.

Any real of hope of repairing the relationship with her mom quickly dissolves. When Jennifer returns home from a seven-mile bike ride to attend a recovery meeting, her mother and sister mock her and offer her a glass of wine to help with the weariness.

Within a few weeks, exhausted in her soul, Jennifer finds herself with a date at a bar ordering just one shot. The next thing she remembers is coming to, being given a case of champagne, and popping the corks until she blacks out again. Eighteen months of sobriety . . . gone.

Bricks Without Straw

The experience of freedom inevitably involves setbacks and frustrations. After Moses first demanded Pharaoh to let God's people go, we read that the ruler of Egypt made things harder on the Israelites: "That same day Pharaoh gave this order to the slave drivers and foremen in charge of the people: 'You are no longer to supply the people with straw for making bricks; let them go and gather their own straw. But require them to make the same number of bricks as before; don't reduce the quota. They are lazy'" (Exodus 5:6–8).

Straw is critical to the process of brick making. By adding volume, strength, and structure to the mud-and-sand mixture, straw allows the bricks to cure more quickly and hold together better. Making bricks without straw is like trying to build a cube out of Tinker Toys without using the little sticks that hold the discs together. You can do it, sort of, but not easily. Nor well.

The book of Exodus shows us that at several critical moments on the road out to freedom, the path gets harder before it gets easier. Pharaoh's command to nix the straw shows us that even slavery can get worse, and the Hebrew people's behavior during their wilderness time shows the ever-present temptation to settle for a familiar life rather than one requiring the risks of dependence, faith, and perseverance. It is the same with the road out of habits and destructive tendencies. We often feel divided and torn because we want to be free, but at the same time we want to avoid additional pain. So our vicious habits can divide and conquer us.

And that was the strategy of Pharaoh—to divide and conquer a people so that they would remain captive. We would be wise to pay attention to his tactics.

- First, he made their lives harder by demanding the same number of bricks without supplying adequate material.
- Second, by appointing Hebrew foremen over the larger population of Hebrew slaves, Pharaoh pitted Hebrew against Hebrew.

Once again, Pharaoh's power strategy seems to make a great deal of sense. A divided Israel would be unable to achieve its ultimate goal of freedom. He took their straw, and the people fell apart.

Sounds way too familiar, doesn't it? As we seek to deal with our destructive habits and behaviors, we take the first steps of our journey to freedom and face the ongoing realities of more pain. Often, the hurt is amplified by the fact that those we love—like the Hebrew masters—are the ones who inflict the pain. We are tempted to give up and retreat into the life we once knew.

Also, as we travel the road to freedom, the destruction we wreaked earlier can catch up with us. We can find ourselves having to deal with fractured relationships, tendencies to fall back into our unhealthy habits, ongoing struggles with issues we thought we had laid to rest, and the weight of emotional baggage.

But in my experience, the early days of recovery presented the most difficulties. When I first surrendered to God and began to experience freedom, all my problems did not disappear. To the contrary, I continually found myself in very tough situations. My life was no longer heading toward the crash. *The crash had happened—and I'd survived.* Now what did I need to do to take the next step?

I needed to:

- Distance myself from the friends I had always partied with.
- Learn how to live sober.
- Discover how to face conflict, challenges, and other

struggles without giving in to destructive patterns. Handling all of that was a huge challenge. After the earthquakes in my past, I had to deal with tons of emotional and relational rubble. I started the hard work of rebuilding, brick by brick.

At such difficult points, when we're exhausted and hurting, we need to understand that, contrary to the power strategy of Pharaoh, God's strategy is one of love. He works mysteriously to empower our journey to freedom. God, for instance, saw Israel's lack of straw *as one more step toward freedom for his people.* This additional hardship made life for the Israelites difficult enough that they *had* to move ahead and outside of the familiar life as slaves. Exodus points us continually to a huge theme of the book: *the people would come to know the Lord.*

The real difficulty for each of us—and for Israel—is trusting that God has a plan and purpose and that he has already orchestrated our deliverance. Life will get tough. We may feel like we are making bricks without straw, but God is teaching us to know him better and to trust him more. Unlike Pharaoh's wishes for the Hebrew people, God wants his people—you and me—to grow and develop. Granted, it can be so frustrating when you make positive decisions and life seems to get worse or more confusing. But I've always grown more spiritually during hard times than good ones. When God takes your straw, it isn't because he wants you to remain a slave. It's because he wants you to take another step toward freedom.

Forging Ahead Despite Detours

Waking up after three days of nonstop drinking, Jennifer returns to her mother's house, stuffs her belongings into her backpacks, collects the eighty dollars remaining to her name, and buys a bus ticket back to California.

She prays repeatedly, asking God for the strength to continue and for his love to sustain her. Unexpectedly, at the oddest times and places, she encounters the kindness of others—sleeping on friends' couches, their arms folded around her in prayers for her continued recovery; a loan of a bicycle to ride to the two jobs she landed within a day of her arrival; and a request from a man in her AA group to watch his apartment while he serves a three-month sentence for an earlier drunk-driving offense. As Jennifer continues to surrender to God, she finds a growing peace and the power to persevere in hope and faith. Things are hard emotionally, financially, and spiritually. But Jennifer is growing and taking the steps, however shaky, that lead out.

When life gets harder, it is normal to want to quit. We want to go back. We romanticize the past and remember what was good about the predictable routines of captivity. Fear causes us to lose our bearings. That's one reason why, in the Sermon on the Mount, Jesus gave this practical advice to his followers: "Do not worry about your life, what you will eat or drink; or about your body, what you will wear . . . Therefore do not worry about tomorrow, for tomorrow will worry about itself. Each day has enough trouble of its own" (Matthew 6:25, 34).

In our journey to overcome whatever holds us back, the essential focus is on today. What are you facing right now? What positive step toward freedom can you choose? What worry do you need to give to God in the light of his promise that he will take care of you?

Twenty years into sobriety, Jennifer recalls the great difficulty and pain of leaving her mother's home so she could continue her recovery: "I had to leave everything behind to follow God's will and direction for my life. In the moment, it is very difficult. You have to make a decision to give up your own will and your control and take that plunge into the ocean, usually having no idea what that will mean. That has been my experience of surrendering. It means to have faith in what you don't know and to trust in God for his direction."

As we walk the broken road toward freedom, the journey gets difficult, and we all need words of encouragement. So train yourself to turn to the truth of the Bible when you face temptation.

I'll never forget hearing Charles Swindoll, a well-known Christian writer and pastor, tell a personal story about resisting temptation. After speaking at a convention, Chuck was in an elevator going back to his room. When two beautiful women got in, they began to flirt with him. It wasn't long before one of them asked, "Would you like a date tonight?" Swindoll was tempted. He was worn out, and he was alone. But in the moment he heard over and over in his mind the words of Galatians 6:7, "Don't be misled—you cannot mock the justice of God. You will always harvest what you plant"

(NLT). Swindoll declined the young woman's offer.

Meditate on the Bible's truths. Let its rich wisdom and insight live in your heart and mind. God's truth will both sustain you in moments of temptation and remind you of the promises he has for you each new day. Don't focus on yesterday or tomorrow; you have today. Settle into each moment. Trust God so you may take another step toward freedom.

Just a Minute

What promise in the Bible is God using to sustain your walk on the broken road, your walk toward freedom? What words of encouragement from God's Word help you put one foot in front of the other? If you need some ideas, take a look at these: Psalm 23; Isaiah 43:1–3; Jeremiah 29:11; Romans 8:38–39; and 1 John 3:1.

Make It Right

When I was a young teenager, I was banned from all Sears stores until I turned eighteen . . .

One day when I was leaving the store, a security guard grabbed my arm and said, "Excuse me. I need to know where you put the cassette tape."

I said, "I didn't put it anywhere. I don't know what you're talking about."

I lied.

He took me to a back room where he searched me and didn't find anything. Then, as his second search was ending, he felt something hidden under my shirt. It was a cassette tape of the eighties band Dokken. I was busted.

When my father was called, I'm pretty sure he encouraged the store to have the police teach me a lesson. In any case, the point was dramatically made: the police came, cuffed me, and walked me out the front door while everyone watched. They put me in a police car and took me to the station. I was terrified.

Even worse than being put in jail, though, would be facing my father. When he picked me up at the police station, he didn't say a word. All the way home in the car, the silence was deafening. Upon our return home, he asked me to sit down in the kitchen. He sat down next to me and looked out the window, still not saying a word. To this day, I remember the sound of the clock ticking. After what seemed like forever, my father finally spoke: "Jud, I don't understand why you would steal. You know better than that. You *are* better than that."

All I could say was "I'm sorry" and offer to somehow make things right with my family and others. After that, my stealing days were over.

That day taught me that the heart of restitution begins with words that can be very difficult to speak: *I'm sorry.* In the years since, I have learned again and again that those words, combined with action to make practical amends, are life transforming. They are words of freedom.

But saying "I'm sorry" is difficult, and one reason is that it requires us to focus on our own responsibility rather than other people's behavior. We all get hurt. In my own life, I can think of a couple people who betrayed my trust and deeply wounded me. I remember the all-consuming anger and bitterness I felt toward them for a long time. Most of us could develop long lists of ways we have been treated unfairly or suffered because of people's words and actions.

- My father was emotionally absent.
- My uncle molested me.
- My mother abandoned our family.
- My boss exploited me.
- My best friend betrayed me.
- My mortgage company ripped me off.
- My children aren't grateful for the sacrifices I've made for them.
- My God has led me into a desert to die.

We've all been hurt, we've all been burned, and we've all been wronged. And the temptation is always to think, "I'll say I'm sorry when he says he's sorry."

There is also the temptation to blame. We may seek to shift *all* of the responsibility for the pain to the one who has hurt us and attempt to inflict at least an equal amount of suffering on that person. The deadly reality plays itself out: hurt people seek to make others pay for their pain.

Part of the healing comes when we take time to consider how many "Who Has Hurt Me" lists our name would appear on. Each of us hurts people and damages relationships. So don't play the blame game because you're as guilty of hurting people as those people you want to blame for hurting you. Instead of blaming, seek to make amends for your own mistakes.

Restitution

During their desert wanderings, God established a way for the Israelites to say, "I'm sorry" not just with words, but with acts of restitution as well. The series of *if-then* scenarios recorded in Exodus 22 reveals God's loving process for enabling us to make things right when we have wronged someone.

God is serious about restitution. In some instances, the amends he requires go beyond the scope of the original offense. A person caught stealing, for instance, is to pay back several times the value of what was stolen. Even more surprising is that God sometimes requires amends even if the crime was unintentional. Exodus 22:6 records, "If a fire breaks out and spreads into thornbushes so that it burns shocks of grain or standing grain or the whole field, the one who started the fire must make restitution."

A fire breaking out is a particular circumstance calling for restitution, but it also serves as a deeper picture of the way damage occurs. Most of the time, we don't intend to hurt the ones we love. Sometimes things—sometimes *we*—just get out of control. We don't mean to neglect our children by allowing the pressure of work to take control of our time. We don't really mean some of what we say to our spouse in a moment of anger. And we rarely see our own blind spots that cause us to protect ourselves and even manipulate others.

By establishing codes for restitution, God acknowledges the ways we wound others. Restitution is the process of making loving attempts to reverse the damage of the hurt we caused either intentionally or unintentionally. Healing comes when we take steps to repair a relationship.

Ultimately, God shows forth his model of restitution most fully in the cross of Jesus. There, Jesus made restitution on our behalf for something he did not do. Furthermore, he is our supreme example of repairing relationships that have been broken, specifically the relationship between sinful human beings and their holy Creator. If we embrace Jesus, then we must also embrace a lifestyle of restitution.

Amends and Forgiveness

After their son's soccer game on a bright Las Vegas afternoon, Shaun hands his Blackberry to his wife without thinking. Opening the browser, she finds her husband's last page—an online advertisement for a paid escort. When he rips the phone from her hands, his truck swerves across the right lane, and they nearly crash. She screams at him to hand it over, but he holds on.

At home, Shaun locks himself in the bathroom and erases all the critical history and deletes certain files in an attempt to try to establish his innocence. As he does so, his wife, screaming in anger, throws framed wedding photos against the bathroom door.

A day or so later, Shaun feels sick and suicidal. He wants to confess but can't imagine how he could keep from losing his family if his wife knew the full truth. Now living in a basement room, he descends into self-hatred stemming from a profound sense of shame.

In a different room of the same house, Lynette's carefully designed plan to build a family totally different from the one she knew growing up—a family that would be free from abuse and addiction—crumbles around her. Struggling with a depression triggered by these discoveries of her husband's infidelities, she realizes that a terrible history of fights, secrets, lies, and addictions is repeating itself. The college degrees, good jobs, and well-landscaped house are a façade, and Lynette wonders what—if anything—lies behind the disguise. She falls apart, overwhelmed by feelings of failure.

At this point in time, Shaun and Lynette share a broken marriage, shattered histories, and a deep longing for change without any hope that change for the better could ever happen. They feel alone in the desert, both literally and figuratively.

Feeling powerless, they both seek help. Shaun is diagnosed as being in the grip of sexual addiction, and Lynette is asked to work through the issues of codependency. They attend a recovery meeting at Central Christian Church and, despite their initial horror at the idea of bringing God into these circumstances, tap into his power. They learn to surrender to him in a way *neither of them could have ever imagined.*

In the aftermath of her heartbreaking discovery about her husband, Lynette is hounded by an unrelenting obsession. She remembers the depths to which she plummeted late one night well after her children and husband (in another room) had fallen asleep. Sitting on the floor of their bedroom, hours into her continuing search of websites and bank accounts for more of her husband's secrets, she listened to the swirl of voices repeating the same questions in her head: Who has he been with? What have they done? How could he do this to me? *Exhausted, shaky, and confused, Lynette let the tears flow—and she vowed to stop hurting herself like this. She had more than enough pain to go around without self-inflicted wounds.*

On an evening months into their recovery, Shaun rehearses the words he plans to say to his wife. As they both work through the Celebrate Recovery principles and steps, Shaun understands the importance of making amends, but how do you convince someone, after a thousand times of saying you're sorry, that this time you really mean it? And if Lynette even listens, what can he do to make it right? Even though he doesn't have answers to those questions, and even though he fears he may put his marriage in greater jeopardy, Shaun trusts God. So he asks his wife if they could talk after they put their children to bed.

As they sit on the living room couch, Shaun finds himself weeping uncontrollably. Through his sobs, he apologizes not only for his betrayal, but also for the other terrible ways his deception caused her pain. He lists all he can remember—and it takes him awhile. He stresses to Lynette that there was nothing she could have done or said to have changed his choices. And then he waits.

And waits.

It's not that Lynette doesn't want to respond. It's just that she can't find the words to acknowledge the supernatural reality she feels in the moment. In her own healing process, she has experienced the love and grace of God, which freed her to work on her own issues—her own anger, shame, and obsessions—instead of trying to fix her husband. As she released Shaun to God's care, she discovered beneath her rage a deep sadness over losing her husband and best friend. After Shaun's confession, it takes Lynette a little time to realize that he has not left one hurt uncovered. Then, forgiving him, she thanks him for his apology and the healing gift that it is to her.

Lynette's forgiveness marks a turning point for Shaun, a man who had descended into the pit of deceit and shame. In his sexual addiction, Shaun rationalized sex with prostitutes on the basis of emotional disconnection from his wife, but now, having walked through the door of Lynette's forgiveness, he experiences—and longs for—genuine intimacy. In his wife's love, Shaun sees the love of Jesus. For a person who had condemned himself to a life without love, Shaun feels as if he has experienced a resurrection.

Shaun works hard to make things right with Lynette. He accepts that it will take time for her to fully trust him again. He knows this will mean being completely open with his cell phone and e-mail, with his time and privacy, but he is willing. No more secrets. No more lies. Depending on Jesus, facing his own struggle, seeking the help of others, and maintaining transparency with his wife, Shaun begins to restore the relationship one step at a time.

A year or so later, Shaun and Lynette renew their marriage vows on a beach in Southern California. As Lynette looks into the faces of fifty or so close friends and family members, she recognizes a woman who had told her that she would one day celebrate their recovery. Lynette smiles at the thought. After the earthquake of a marriage broken by infidelity and addiction, she could see nothing except pain for the longest time, but now she begins to see what the woman meant. When desperation leads people to God, the options narrow to two: faith or self-destruction. Choosing faith means choosing an honesty that requires both grace and an ongoing surrender to God marked by dependence on him. Having both sought forgiveness and extended it to each other, Shaun and Lynette renew their vows: God will now be at the center of their marriage, the center of their life.

The Urgency of Forgiveness

The kind of forgiveness demonstrated by Shaun and Lynette occurs over time, and it's a process requiring the repeated use of the *S* and the *F* words: "I'm sorry" and "I forgive you." Sometimes people forgive too quickly and easily without first really grieving the hurt, feeling the anger, and working through the process with God. At the other extreme, if you have held anger or some other negative emotion inside for years, get some help. Don't be afraid of Christian counseling. Work through any underlying issues and whatever pain you're feeling, because you will experience tremendous freedom on the other side.

Although the process of forgiveness takes time, Jesus taught that there is a great urgency about forgiveness. He said that reconciliation is important enough to drop whatever you are doing to seek forgiveness and healing within a relationship (Matthew 5:23–24). Sometimes you have to put one foot in front of the other and just do it, even though you don't feel the desire to do so or you'd rather play the blame game and excuse yourself from any responsibility for the situation.

Be willing to offer forgiveness—and be willing to seek forgiveness. Choose to take the important risk of saying, "I'm sorry" and "I forgive you."

Just a Minute

An important step on your journey to freedom is to make a list of people you have hurt. After you make that list, then list people who have hurt you. Now, reminded of your own need for forgiveness, humbly seek that forgiveness (say, "I'm sorry"). At the same time do the work you need to do to be able to say, "I forgive you" wherever necessary.

8

Let God Fight for You

Newly homeless, Jeff scans the block. Calculating in his head the distance necessary for a driver to see him and then stop, he pitches what remains of his possessions on that precise spot halfway down the block. He needs a way out if all else fails him.

Surrendering to the last of his drugs—an IV fuse of cocaine and heroin—Jeff lifts one final desperate prayer: "Please end the pain." He prays to Jesus, but he isn't certain why.

Before his parents' divorce and his plunge into emotional and physical poverty, Jeff was drawn to the reality of Jesus. As a child and then as an altar boy in training, he spent hours in the dark, standing in front of a lonely altar, searching the face of Jesus, and wondering why a Man would willingly put himself in the place of such suffering.

Years later, on the day of his release from yet another rehabilitation sentence, Jeff asks Jesus to save him. But two hours later he is back on the street with another needle in a pockmarked vein. Yet even at this moment of retreat back into his old habits, Jeff feels the reality of a love that pursues him. Helpless addict that he is, Jeff nevertheless understands that Jesus is somehow fighting for him.

At the same time Jeff lifts another simple prayer to Jesus —"Help!"—he rehearses his plan in his mind one more time: step, step, step, a loud horn, squealing brakes, and then a thud. And his pain would be over.

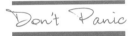

Don't Panic

In the story of Exodus, God cast Israel as the ultimate underdog. He chose Moses, a shepherd and murderer, to lead a captive people into a showdown with the king of the world's largest empire. The point of the narrative: God's glory remains unstoppable. His power fuels redemption, and his grace allows us to receive it.

You are asked to believe.

Imagine the odds against the underdog Israel. Thousands and thousands of troops—part of Egypt's state-of-the-art war machine—descended in chariots and horses while the raging

Red Sea blocked the Hebrews' only escape. Can you imagine the fear and desperation?

Exodus 14:13–14 picks up the story: "Moses answered the people, 'Do not be afraid. Stand firm and you will see the deliverance the LORD will bring you today. The Egyptians you see today you will never see again. The LORD will fight for you; you need only to be still.'"

As his people journeyed out of Egypt, God led them into an apparent corner. Apart from a supernatural work of God, they had no hope. So Moses pointed the people to the Almighty, basically saying, "Be still and God will fight for you."

In other words, don't panic.

"Don't panic"? Really?

Awhile back someone e-mailed me a news item about what to do just in case you are ever in the heart of the Amazon and manage to get yourself swallowed by an anaconda (the largest of snakes, often growing up to thirty-five feet long and capable of swallowing whole a four-hundred-pound animal). These are the steps you should take:

- If you are attacked by an anaconda, don't run. The snake is faster than you are.

- Lie flat on the ground. Put your arms tight against your sides and your legs tight against one another.
- Tuck in your chin.
- Do not panic, but the snake will begin to nudge and climb over your body.
- After the snake has examined you, it will begin to swallow you from the feet in, always from the feet in. Permit the snake to swallow your feet and ankles. Do not panic.
- The snake will now begin to suck your legs into its body. You must lie perfectly still. This will take a long time.
- When the snake has reached your knees, slowly and with as little movement as possible, reach down to get your knife and very gently slide it into the snake's mouth between the edge of its mouth and your leg. Suddenly rip upwards, severing its head.

Don't panic? Give me a break.

The Glory of God

Israel cried out to God in panic: "Was it because there were no graves in Egypt that you brought us to the desert to die? What have you done to us by bringing us out of Egypt? Didn't we say to you in Egypt, 'Leave us alone; let us serve the Egyptians'? It would have been better for us to serve the Egyptians than to die in the desert!" (Exodus 14:11–12).

Again, here is the reality of choosing the certainty of slavery over the promise of freedom. Israel was a people who should've known better. They had witnessed a series of devastating plagues that brought Egypt to its knees, but Israel still found it difficult to trust God. Through Moses, God instructed the people to stand still and watch what he would do. Let there be no mistake about it: the redemption of his people and the world would become a reality as a result of God's invincible power and the carefully planned movement of his glory.

Remember Moses' response to God's panicky people? "Do not be afraid. Stand firm . . . The LORD will fight for you; you need only to be still'" (verses 13–14). These commands to not be afraid and to stand still often appear in Old Testament military scenes. In this case, the battle lines were drawn: Israel was on one side and Egypt on the other. Israel was facing an overwhelming Egyptian army with its far superior military technology.

The only chance of victory belonged to God.

Be still so that God alone gets the glory.

God's glory is intimately connected to our deliverance. God weaves his plan into the details of human life. Way too often we forget that when God tells us to wait, he doesn't do so to burn some time but to reveal his supernatural activity in the context of our lives. He tells us to wait, so that we can clearly see him do the work.

God loves the patient faith of an underdog.

Wait or Act?

Do you ever feel like an underdog? Does it seem that nothing ever goes your way, that life is difficult at best, even impossible at times? Take heart. The good news of the work of Jesus, accomplished as he suffered on the cross, is that the odds have been reversed. In the end, the underdogs win.

I admit to a fondness for the *Rocky* movies. After the first time Sylvester Stallone yelled out, "Yo, Adrian," I bought a punching bag and hung it in the shed behind our house in the unlikely hopes of becoming a boxer. That didn't happen, but I was lucky enough to screen the final movie of the series, *Rocky Balboa*, with a small group of people that included star Sylvester Stallone. When asked about biblical themes running through the movies, Stallone pointed to the first scene of the first movie, which shows a painting of Jesus. The camera then panned down to reveal an old church transformed into a rundown boxing ring. As Balboa slugged it out from the bottom of his life and his career, Jesus stood above him, with the word *Resurrection* painted on the wall behind the ring. Rocky had a destiny to fulfill, and even though he was a broken guy who was totally down on his luck—a symbol of the ultimate underdog—God was not finished with him or with the final story line.

Like Rocky and Israel, we must act and not just wait. In the paradox of the gospel, redemption finds its path along the line of an individual's active faith. Check out the sense of irony in God's response to the plea of Israel: "Then the

Lord said to Moses, 'Why are you crying out to me? Tell the Israelites to move on'" (Exodus 14:15). Moses already knew what to do: go to the edge of the Red Sea, lift up his staff, and get this thing moving.

In Scripture, we often find tension between waiting and acting. Some people say they wait on the Lord when they are merely being lazy. (And just as we can fail by not acting, we can fail by not waiting.)

If you have an issue with bitterness or anger toward another person, you aren't to avoid a conversation in favor of staying in your closet to pray. God says, "I'll work and you can watch me work, but you need to participate through faith in what I am doing."

With the Egyptians in close pursuit, the Israelites ran as hard as they could to the very edge of the Red Sea—and God rescued them. The sea swallowed the Egyptians.

This is a great salvation moment in Israel's history—and here in Exodus 14 is the first time the word *save* is used in the Bible. This Hebrew word is reserved almost exclusively for the work of God. It is through his grace that we get in on it.

Party Time

On the other side of the Red Sea, a free people celebrated. They sang out to God:

> I will sing to the LORD,
>   for he is highly exalted.
> The horse and its rider
>   he has hurled into the sea.
> The LORD is my strength and my song;
>   he has become my salvation.
> He is my God, and I will praise him,
>   my father's God, and I will exalt him. Exodus 15:1–2

Moses acknowledged that the Lord had won the victory, and now his people celebrated with a song that focuses on God's power and mighty deliverance. When God's people see his mercy, the result is elation, praise, and joy. Israel had seen God move. They couldn't help but shout for joy. God is the focus of this song because of what he has done.

The celebration reverberates into eternity. Revelation 5:9 declares Jesus worthy of praise because he "purchased men for God from every tribe and language and people and nation." That invitation opens up God's party to all of us.

We respond to God's activity on our behalf with heartfelt worship and joyous praise. When we celebrate our victories—whether it's another day sober or a restored relationship—our joy does not focus on what we have done, but rather on what Christ has done on our behalf.

On the curb downhill from the bus station, Jeff takes one step, and then another, and then another with the same precision he has practiced during two hopeless years on the street. After taking his last step, he runs into some kind of invisible object that knocks him backward, out of the path of the bus. He feels like he has walked into a sliding-glass door.

As Jeff rises, stunned and angry, he cries out to God, "I can't take this anymore! Either help me or kill me, God, because I am broken! I am at the end of myself!"

In a place deeper down than his rage, Jeff senses a power moving through his powerlessness, beyond his fear and hate, and as he surrenders, a spark nestles into his soul. That evening, when Jeff finds his way to the Las Vegas Rescue Mission for a bite to eat, God places in his path a mission resident who leads him into a Steps Recovery program.

And Jeff writes about the moment in his journal so he can continually celebrate the work of God, who does for him what he can't do for himself.

Two years into his sobriety, Jeff experiences a life of joy and purpose far greater than he ever would have imagined having. He points to his personal paraphrase of the text of Psalm 107 to describe his new life of thanksgiving:

Let's give thanks to the Lord for his unfailing love and his wonderful deeds for men, for he satisfies the thirsty and fills the hungry with good things. Some sat in darkness and the deepest gloom, prisoners suffering in iron chains, for they rebelled against the words of God and despised the counsel of the Most High, so he subjected them to bitter labor; they stumbled, and there was no one to help. Then they cried to the Lord in their trouble, and he saved them from their distress. He brought them out of darkness and the deepest gloom *and broke away their chains. Let them give thanks to the Lord for his unfailing love and his wonderful deeds for men.*

In response to God's remarkable and supernatural intervention, Jeff acts. He works through each step in his recovery program, seeks to make amends to the people he has hurt, and takes seriously his responsibility to move forward in his recovery. But this time what motivates his actions is different from his many earlier efforts to find healing. What was missing, Jeff says, was any knowledge of God's love. As God continues to work in Jeff's heart and life a recovery beyond Jeff 's own power, he understands that God does so out of love—and that truth blows Jeff away. Aware of and amazed by God's love, Jeff finds himself not so much acting on his own behalf but responding to God's love by extending grace to others. As Jeff comes to grips with God's forgiveness, he responds by forgiving himself and others.

Jeff now helps lead the recovery program at our church, and he has also been involved with a ministry to the homeless. "I have a relationship with Jesus today that is priceless. I know this journey through recovery is a lifelong process, and I still battle against my own desires to serve myself. But what's different today is that I know I'm not alone. I know God loves me.

When times get rough, which they do, I go to God. I contact people, share how I feel, and work through situations, not run from them. My life has meaning. I have peace, not pain, and I've become willing to let God work through me to reach out and help the one who is suffering."

Just a Minute

Celebrate what God has done on your behalf. Thank him that you're on the journey to know him better, a journey to be free. Celebrate, too, the truth that "if the Son sets you free, you will be free indeed" (John 8:36).

9

Ditch the Loner Routine

Mark's plan to do a Nicolas Cage and leave Las Vegas runs smoothly until a certain point. The idea of a man drinking himself to death takes on a strange appeal for Mark, who is forty-two and feels he has no options. Leaving a woman who still loves him and two children who consider it no big loss, Mark checks into a Las Vegas apartment and—according to his plan—furnishes it with nothing other than a sleeping bag and refrigerator. In his mind, as the police kneel over him, he expects one of them to say that it's just another suicide stiff.

Sick to death of the carnage from decades of addiction, of running from everything and everyone, Mark sits night after night in his apartment, his back leaning against the bedroom wall, drinking until he blacks out. Sometimes in the mornings when he comes to, he doesn't recognize where he is. More often, though, Mark thinks to himself, Damn, I'm still here. And I'm all alone.

Arms Held Up

God does not intend for us to live our lives in isolation. We are not designed to be loners.

On their way out of Egypt, for example, God's people lived and moved as a community. After encountering the Amalekites, who vowed Israel's destruction, the people teamed together for battle in a way that revealed their need for God and for one another. As Joshua led the troops out in war, Aaron and Hur stayed with Moses. Exodus 17:10–12 reads:

> So Joshua fought the Amalekites as Moses had ordered, and Moses, Aaron and Hur went to the top of the hill. As long as Moses held up his hands, the Israelites were winning, but whenever he lowered his hands, the Amalekites were winning. When Moses' hands grew tired, they took a stone and put it under him and he sat on it. Aaron and Hur held his hands up—one on one side, one on the other—so that his hands remained steady till sunset.

We can't win life's battles on our own. We can't find freedom alone. Even with God on his side, Moses needed people to walk with him and to hold his arms up. Moses needed flesh-and-blood human beings who would encourage him and pray with him. So do we.

Becoming free and staying free from the stuff that holds us back is never an isolated thing. Becoming free and staying free happens in community with the help and encouragement of others. So one of the most important ways to stay free is to build strong relationships with people who are positive and life giving, people who encourage you to make wise decisions and who cheer for you when you do.

When I realized my life was crazy and unmanageable, I reached out to God, but I would have never made it if it weren't for a small group of people at my local church who loved me and cared for me. God used them to save my life. That was more than twenty years ago, but the same principles hold true for me today. I stay free and I keep growing because of the relationships in my life. The small group of people who challenge me and walk with me are invaluable to my personal and spiritual growth.

The point of desperation brings about an openness to such community. People who are helpless are often more willing to seek out another's help. Believers form a community united by their brokenness; dedicated to loving, supporting, helping, and advocating for one another; and sharing faith that human beings can change and grow in the grace, love, and power of Jesus.

I love the imagery of Moses extending his arms in prayer to God and depending on his brothers to enable him to continue in his obedience to God and his praying for his people. For me, it's a picture of community.

Seeing Jesus

When Mark shows up at a recovery group, Sherman recognizes the look of a beaten person—suicidal, isolated, given over to shame and bitterness. A few years ago, he was that person. So Sherman gives Mark the kind of hug that takes your breath away, and before Mark knows it, Sherman is leading him in a prayer to accept Jesus into his life. Mark is struck by the sense then—as he has been struck at critical points during his suicide plan—that maybe there's another way.

As they talk together afterward, Sherman reassures Mark that he's not alone and shares the story of how he finally said,

"Enough." After his own suicide attempt and weeks into his sobriety, when his ride back from an AA meeting cancelled on him, Sherman had called an old friend, a cook for his former dealer, who drove him to a crystal-meth lab. After nineteen years of drug addiction—eight caught in the insanity of smoking meth— Sherman smelled the meth on the way back from the bathroom and knew how much he wanted it. At that moment he feared for his soul, so he ran outside, praying, "Dear God, please help me. I don't want this anymore, and I don't want to lose my little girl."

When the dealer came out to talk with him, Sherman told him no. Back home in the shower, Sherman got sick the way he used to with drugs. Then he questioned what was different this time from the thousands of other times he had tried to say no and failed.

What was different? It was God, Sherman tells Mark, and Mark knows what he means.

Truth be told, Mark doesn't care too much for Sherman initially. This pushing Jesus right in his face and telling him he needed to say this prayer—it makes Mark dislike him because of Sherman's exclusive claim on loud-mouthed arrogance. At the same time, Mark feels this mysterious draw and keeps showing up for something that just might be there.

Sherman becomes Mark's sponsor, and there are some days when Mark wishes he could talk about baseball or the weather. Working through the Steps Recovery program with Mark, Sherman seeks to engage Mark in the most difficult challenge of recovery—helping Mark see the truth about himself. He challenges Mark to do the hard work of repenting, seeking forgiveness, making amends, and telling the truth—in the context of the grace of Jesus, whom Mark genuinely begins to see in Sherman's friendship and love. As Mark works on making amends for his lifestyle of addiction, he meets with Sherman in a park and reveals a number of dark secrets.

Over and over he hears this from Sherman and the community of churchgoers around him: "Good news, dude! Jesus has you covered!"

On the evening of Mark's baptism in front of thousands of people, he's nervous about standing before such a large crowd. Sherman tells Mark it's not about the crowd or, for that matter, about Jesus this time. "It's about you," he says. "Through your baptism, you are telling the world about God's grace, about God's ability to redeem a life."

Sherman baptizes Mark, and when he surfaces from under the water, instead of Sherman's face, Mark sees Jesus. A few seconds later, Sherman looks at Mark with that overly confident smile and asks him, "You saw Jesus, too, didn't you?"

Keep Showing Up

Sometimes when people make a decision for Christ, they corner me and say, "I've made this decision. I've been baptized. What do I need to do now?" When I don't have time to give them the long answer, I give them this three-word short version: "Keep showing up." Some people protest: they want something more specific like a training course or something more difficult like a commitment to going a year without chocolate. Do you know what I've learned? Life really is 90 percent about showing up. Hebrews 10:24–25 argues for the reality of community: "Let us not give up meeting together, as some are in the habit of doing, but let us encourage one another—and all the more as you see the Day approaching." The early believers stayed connected to one another.

So, keep showing up. Keep showing up before God in prayer and Bible study. Keep showing up and spending time with encouraging friends. Keep showing up at church.

Because when you show up, God moves. He is going to work in your life through his community and grow you in a way you could never experience on your own.

To celebrate their continuing recovery, Mark and Sherman's community group rents a cabin on Panguitch Lake in Utah. Nine adults—and a bunch of children—gather for the second straight year. Having spent at least three years together, the group comes together in ways that have become natural to them. Recovering addicts, previously isolated and alienated, now openly share with one another their ongoing struggles, fears, and hopes. They have learned what it means to have a brother or sister, and they are uncles and aunts for one another's kids. By the grace and power of God, they have overcome great odds. Now they share in a deep response of worship and wonder. They continue to show up for one another.

On the second day of the retreat—Independence Day—Mark feels the need to clear his head after dinner. As he fires up an ATV, Sherman happens along and asks Mark, "Mind if I join you?"

Just before the road becomes a path into the woods, Sherman requests a trade of four-wheelers; he prefers the manual transmission. They make the exchange, and Mark watches as his friend heads out first. As Sherman begins to climb the short uphill grade, he glances back with a look that says he's not going to make it. The horror seems to unfold in slow motion, and Mark watches Sherman go up and the four-wheeler overturn and drop him fifteen feet to the ground.

When Mark reaches him, Sherman says, "I'm messed up." He can't move his arms or legs. His face is in the dirt and he can't breathe, so Mark digs a hole beside his mouth and nose. With the little air he can manage, Sherman prays: "Please, God, help me be okay."

After the ambulance leaves, Mark stays behind with the police. When the necessary paperwork is completed and the police leave, Mark stands alone in the middle of the darkening woods. He wonders about what has happened. He feels alone and isolated. Fearing that his best friend might be paralyzed below the neck or dying, Mark yells out, "Where were you, God?" Even more intense than the fear, Mark feels shaken by his inability to do anything to help. He prays for ways to love his brother Sherman.

Hours later, shortly before his transfer from Utah to a Las Vegas hospital, C-scan tests are conducted on Sherman, who has become nauseous. Strapped down to the table, unable to move anything below his neck, Sherman turns to Mark and asks him to sing a song.

"Blessed Be the Name of the Lord" is the first song that comes to Mark's mind, and that's what he sings to his friend. In the shared community of pain, hope, and dependence, Sherman can't feel Mark's hand on his, but he knows it's there.

In the wake of Sherman's accident, Mark often feels powerless to help much, but he continues to practice the words of his mentor that proved critical to his own recovery: "Just keep showing up." By sitting in hospital waiting rooms and phoning the rehab facilities and showing up whenever he can with a joke, a story, a word of encouragement, or a prayer, Mark provides healing to his friend in ways he doesn't understand.

Just a Minute

What was the hardest thing for you about moving from "Loner" to "Member of Community"—and what was the best result of taking that risk? If you haven't yet made that move, figure out why you haven't. What will you do to encourage yourself to take that step and/or reward yourself once you do?

10

Guard Your Heart

Okay, I admit it. I'm a closet reality-TV fan.

It's not something I'm proud of. I mean, come on! Reality TV is shallow, it's a waste of time, and it's mindless . . . but I *like* it! Actually, my wife watches, and I get drawn in. When a reality show is on, I'll sit in the living room with my computer as if I'm working, but I position myself so that I can see the TV. Once I'm hooked, I'm addicted for the run of the show. One of the lowest moments in my adult life happened when I rescheduled an appointment so I could get home to see the final episode of *The Bachelorette*.

You kind of lose respect for me as a pastor, don't you?

One of my favorite reality shows is *American Idol*. I love to see ordinary people whose whole lives are changed by their appearance on the show. And I'm a voter. I call in my picks just like millions of other Americans.

The reality for Americans is that we love our idols.

Good Idols Are the Worst

From a biblical standpoint, an idol is anything that takes our attention away from worshiping the one true God. But we are often quick to make people, stuff, hobbies, or addictions more important than God. When we do so, we begin to drift away from the path to freedom. If we are going to stay free, it is crucial that we guard our hearts and keep God first.

For the longest time, Molly's recovery is fueled by fear. She puts off taking a personal inventory because she is certain that she wouldn't be able to stand the pain from too much heartbreak, from the rubble and litter of broken lives. Sober for eight years, she is, however, building a recovery driven by fear. A head-on collision with another drunk driver suggests there's a deeper problem. But the shame, rooted in the times she sold herself for drugs, is too much for her. She believes it would kill her to have to go back there.

So, even as she enters ministry as an assistant to those in recovery, Molly takes the remaining steps of her recovery on the weak backs of good idols—in order: sobriety, ministry, food, and her relationship with her husband.

And it's her husband who is now causing the problem. Beginning a seventy-two-week chemotherapy treatment for exposure to Agent Orange in the Vietnam War, her once-caring husband has retreated into a despondency resulting in abusive and delusional behavior. Her constant fear that she will find him dead in the basement leads Molly to eat everything in sight. When a friend suggests she revisit the idea of a personal inventory, she responds that it's her husband's fault.

Molly thinks she is doing okay—eight years sober and giving herself for the cause that saved her life. And then comes the chaos of her husband's chemotherapy and the toxic sludge he leaves in her life. Fearing his suicide, she breaks down, eats up, and finds it necessary to take a break from her ministry job. Molly watches each of her idols crumbling before her in a slow-motion death.

So Molly seeks help and enters another Steps Recovery program. When she finally summons the courage to take a personal inventory of her life, the pain she experiences is no less than what she had imagined and feared. At one point, she calls a friend to ask for help but manages only a series of uncontrollable sobs. Molly believes she won't hold up in the overwhelming flood of pain and regret but understands that continued healing *requires a renewed perspective on her relationship with God. Out of his love, God supplies the power to change. She is finally willing to bank her life on it.*

After weeping into the phone to her friend, Molly sees her husband differently. Instead of seeing him as a monster degrading her with his moods and post-traumatic spells, she sees the man she loves struggling with his own issues. She no longer insists upon his growth before hers, and she grants him the freedom to suffer alone. She no longer feels responsible for fixing his pain. She also checks into a weight-loss program, loses sixty pounds, and no longer turns to food to numb her pain. By working through her past, seeking forgiveness, and making amends when possible, she begins the process of replacing fear with love.

At one point during her husband's chemotherapy treatment, Molly receives a text message while she is sitting in her home office. It's from her husband who is sitting in the living room: "Why aren't you checking in on me?" Thinking back to the days of her codependence, when she was overwhelmed by her husband's abusive and often delusional behavior, Molly recognizes this as an opportunity to fall deeper into guilt and feelings of helplessness. Instead she walks straight into the living room, looks her husband in the eye, smiles, and says, "How am I supposed to get better if you don't give me the room to do so?"

As part of her own recovery, Molly is learning to truly love others without staking her own value on the results of her love for them. She also eats less, prays more, and finds increasing freedom in God.

Drifting from the Path

The Israelites were free. They had watched God miraculously work to free them from their bondage in Egypt. They had crossed the Red Sea. God had given them commandments straight from his heart telling them how to live their lives. Having this kind of history with the Almighty, these guys would never drift from the path of God's freedom, right?

Yet Exodus 32 tells the tragic story of Israel's readiness to craft an idol to worship instead of worshiping God. Moses had been on the mountain for forty days and nights where he received God's law and instructions about the tabernacle, the place God promised to inhabit with his presence. One of the lowest points in the Exodus story immediately follows

Moses' mountaintop experience with God. Apparently, Israel suffered from corporate attention deficit disorder.

Israel was ready to be like the other nations they'd heard about: Israel wanted to worship a god they could see, and that meant worshiping an idol. They forgot to take an honest inventory of their journey with God. As a result, their desert diet of manna became boring. Water coming out of rocks seemed passé. God guiding them with miraculous signs in the sky looked pyrotechnic. That Red Sea bit was impressive when it happened, but those Egyptians really were overrated as chariot drivers. In its corporate crafting of a handmade idol, Israel denied the power, grace, and love of God made evident when he set them free.

After all, who *was* this God who had led them into a desert—and where was he now? And wasn't it time to worship a god that had some kind of physical form and could be depended on to show up? Even Moses' brother, Aaron, yielded to the people's demands. Exodus 32:4 picks up the story: "He took what they handed him and made it into an idol cast in the shape of a calf, fashioning it with a tool. Then they said, 'These are your gods, O Israel, who brought you up out of Egypt.'"

In the agricultural society of this ancient world, bulls were a symbol of strength and fertility. It was also very common for people to create a physical representation of their gods. It only follows, then, that once they got their idol, the Israelites engaged in "revelry," an Old Testament term with definite sexual connotations (verse 6).

Here's the problem: Israel's desire to worship false gods ran directly counter to God's miraculous and loving work of liberating his people from Egypt. Freedom from Egypt should have also meant freedom from idols. But over and over we read that Israel pined for the good old days in Egypt: "Bring on the idols! Bring on the slavery!"

Can you imagine such a thing?

Surface Idols and Deep Idols

We twenty-first-century folks like to craft idols that are a bit more subtle, but we are building them all the same. In our fallen condition, we human beings tend to worship only what we can control. Tim Keller makes a helpful distinction between a surface idol and a deep idol. A surface idol is a means to a deeper idol, which will demand ultimate allegiance. A surface idol often appears initially as a pattern of behavior or an unhealthy concept. For instance, a woman always has to have a boyfriend and feels worthless at the thought of being single. An overbearing father puts pressure on his children to perform so that he can know his neighbors' respect. A businessman works long, unhealthy hours because he is addicted to the approval of others. A funny person craves being the center of attention in order to feel validated. Prompting us to worship surface idols are deep cravings for significance, comfort, security, meaning, approval, and, ultimately, love.

When we lose sight of the power, grace, and love of God, those deep cravings drive us toward addiction to the idols we desire to control. Keller said, "Jesus must become more beautiful to your imagination, more attractive to your heart, than your idol. If you uproot the idol and fail to 'plant' the love of Christ in its place, the idol will grow back."[1]

To remain free, we must continually examine our life and take an honest personal inventory of our values, goals, motives, and actions. If the people of Israel had looked honestly at themselves, they would have understood more clearly their relationship with God and his exclusive claim on their lives. If Israel had been more focused on God's love and grace, poured out bountifully on them during the exodus, a substitute god would never do.

Clearly, Israel's relationship with God needed repair. Because of the golden-calf episode, God had to withdraw his intimate presence from his people. It would be a violation of God's holiness to remain intimately connected to people who treat his character as if it were worthless.

God chose Moses to lead Israel for several reasons, not the least of which was his deep desire for the presence of God. Moses therefore offered the antidote for Israel's ongoing temptation to craft idols and recurring desire to return to captivity in Egypt, and that antidote was Moses' heartfelt desire for a loving relationship with God. In his own life, Moses desired God's presence, and in response God revealed more and more of himself. God revealed himself to Moses in mysterious and amazing ways, but none more amazing than this particular moment recorded in Exodus: "'I will cause all my goodness to pass in front of you, and I will proclaim my name, the LORD, in your presence . . . But,' he said, 'you cannot see my face, for no one may see me and live'" (Exodus 33:19–20).

Hiding in the cleft of a rock, Moses experienced God's overwhelming mercy and graciousness as the Almighty chose to reveal a bit of his consuming glory to this faithful servant.

Moses longed for the presence of God, and God responded to his desire. Moses longed for the people he was leading to thirst for God's presence as well.

Healing the Rift

In the same way that the sin of idolatry broke Israel's relationship with God, our pain, brokenness, negative habits, and addictions short-circuit the intimacy with God that we, too, desire. We long for God's presence in our lives, and the experience of that mysterious joy comes only with the renewal of our relationship with God. Like Moses, we will then find ourselves seeking the presence of God in prayer, in meditation, and in a growing intimacy with him—which is exactly what God desires to have with us.

Just a Minute

When we pursue an idol, we deny the character of God. Our actions reveal doubts like these: *Does he really love me? Will he really take care of me? Can he really be trusted?* So examine the idols of your own making. Who or what are you placing before God in your life? Acknowledge that and ask God to help you live with him at the center of your life.

11

Live Out Loud

Months after the accident that left him paralyzed from the neck down, Sherman finds himself facing his worst fear—not a continuing physical paralysis, but a spiritual one. He feels he may be losing God. Up through the weekend of the July 4 retreat with his friends, Sherman felt that God had always been in the business of protecting him, miraculously rescuing him from years of addiction, sending his mom over just after he had taken bottles of sleeping pills, and giving him the courage to say no to his meth dealer after a seven-year habit. You just can't explain these kinds of things.

Then, during the time of celebration before his accident, Sherman realized the life-giving power of his community of friends, who surrounded him, prayed for him, and loved him. What a gift from God! Having known a life filled with alienation, chaos, and destruction, Sherman saw God transforming his life, day by day and moment by moment, into one of purpose and service.

But once the four-wheeler flipped over, throwing him fifteen feet to the ground and severing his spine between C5 and C6, Sherman begins to feel more distant from the God he had come to know. It isn't as much an issue of anger as fear: "If I can't count on God to protect me, who can I count on?"

At the depth of Sherman's doubt, Mark shows up, as he has frequently, to pray for healing for his best friend. Sherman shares his fear and together, for the first time, they sort through the circumstances following his accident. Miles into the darkening woods with no one around and no cell phone reception, they heard the voice of a man, who happened to be a paramedic, who managed to call for an ambulance. Five-and-a-half hours later, Sherman was in the operating room under the skilled care of one of the country's best spinal cord surgeons. When the doctor told Sherman's wife that her husband was leaking spinal cord fluid into his lungs and that he was too unstable for another surgery, she asked everyone in the waiting room to pray. Within minutes, his condition stabilized.

In an induced coma for forty-five days, Sherman nearly died twice, but he then awoke without a trace of brain damage. He was, however, given a firm prognosis for life without any movement below his neck. The next stop was a Denver rehabilitation center ranked third in the nation. Then Sherman returned home five months after his injury with feeling in his toes and ankles and some control of his arms.

So when Sherman vows to Mark that, by God's continued grace, he hopes to walk again, they smile at each other. Together they recognize God's loving protection of Sherman following his accident. As Mark prays for his friend, Sherman realizes that God's ongoing healing is not just physical but deeply spiritual as well.

The Glory of God

In the book of Exodus, God set in motion plans for the tabernacle, the site of his promised presence in the midst of his people. Exodus 40:34 records the consummation of the work: "The Cloud covered the Tent of Meeting, and the Glory of God filled The Dwelling" (MSG).

Can you imagine the moment? Think of how Steven Spielberg or James Cameron might imagine it: God in a hovering cloud by day, fire by night. Radiant and pulsing, casting long shadows into the wilderness, the glory of God animated the tabernacle.

Still on the outskirts of the Promised Land, Israel was already familiar with God's glory—in the pillar of fire and the cloud that protected them from Egypt's armies; in the miracle of the parting of the Red Sea; and in the fire on the distant heights of Mount Sinai. But none of that compares to the weight, the power, and the light of the Divine filling the tabernacle. I love how one commentator describes this: "The God of the exodus—the God of power, who made the heavens and the earth; the God of justice, who plagued the Egyptians; the God of love, who kept his covenant with Israel; the God of providence, who led his people through the wilderness; the God of truth, who gave them his law; the God of mercy, who atoned for their sins; the God of holiness, who set them apart for service—this great God was present in glory."[1]

The climax of the book of Exodus is God indwelling the tabernacle. During Israel's four hundred years of slavery, God occasionally revealed himself, and when he did so, he radically changed the situation. In Exodus 25–40, God shared his plans for the tabernacle, the residence for his glory. He gave his people a series of instructions about construction, design, offerings, ordinances, building materials, and surroundings.

While the glory of God provides reason enough for worship, the fact that God indwelled his tabernacle becomes more amazing in light of several realities. Consider these facts:

- The tabernacle stood in the midst of God's people.

I love Eugene Peterson's translation for *tabernacle* in *The Message*: "dwelling." The tabernacle was not built on a mountain or in a jeweled palace but in the midst of God's people as they wandered in the wilderness. By residing within the community of Israel, God demonstrated that he not only came to save his people but ultimately to be in relationship with them. God chose Israel to be his people, and he made his home with them because of his great love for them. God displayed his glory and power in the world's greatest demonstration of shock and awe, not just for display but to benefit his people.

- The tabernacle was a concrete reality for God's people.

The verb translated "filled" in Exodus 40:34 is significant because it reflects an ongoing, dynamic reality. It denotes not a one-time event—that God filled the tabernacle once and for all—but that God was continually filling the tabernacle, that each moment he was renewing his glory. In addition to indicating the present-tense reality of God, the tabernacle was also portable. This large tent was moved from one place to the next. God was therefore able to lead his people to freedom even as he remained in their midst.

- The tabernacle foreshadowed God's greater dwelling with his people in the person of Jesus.

The tabernacle foreshadowed an even greater revelation of God's glory for the sake of humankind. In the person of Jesus, "God was pleased to have all his fullness dwell in him" (Colossians 1:19), who, in turn, "made his dwelling among us" (John 1:14). *The Message*'s translation of John 1:14 states the reality in contemporary terms:

> The Word became flesh and blood,
> and moved into the neighborhood.
> We saw the glory with our own eyes,
> the one-of-a-kind glory,

like Father, like Son,
Generous inside and out,
true from start to finish.

By God's power and grace and love, we are free.

So now what? Paul wrote, "So Christ has truly set us free. Now make sure that you stay free, and don't get tied up again in slavery" (Galatians 5:1 NLT).

We must not be like Israel, often pining for the familiar routines of captivity, or the early Christians who were tempted to retreat back into the heartless humming of the law. Instead, we believers today must desire to stay free in the ongoing grace of Jesus.

We must resist the temptations of old habits built on the deceptions of self-fulfillment.

If we really believe God dwells with us in power and glory, we can be freed of our obsession with self and instead live in love for others.

As Jesus put it, "Whoever wants to save his life will lose it, but whoever loses his life for me and for the gospel will save it" (Mark 8:35). True life blossoms when we share the love and grace of God with one another.

Living Out Loud

In *The Ragamuffin Gospel*, one of my favorite books, Brennan Manning wrote this:

> Because salvation is by grace through faith, I believe . . . I shall see the prostitute from the Kit-Kat Ranch in Carson City, Nevada, who tearfully told me she could find no other employment to support her two-year-old son. I shall see the woman who had an abortion and is haunted by guilt and remorse but did the best she could faced with grueling alternatives; the businessman besieged with debt who sold his integrity in a series of desperate transactions; the insecure clergyman addicted to being liked, who never challenged his people from the pulpit and longed for unconditional love; the sexually abused teen molested by his father and now selling his body on the street, who, as he falls asleep each night after his last "trick," whispers the name of the unknown God he learned about in Sunday school; the deathbed convert who for decades had his cake and ate it, broke every law of God and man, wallowed in

lust, and raped the earth . . . If this is not good news to you, you have never understood the gospel of grace.[2]

Along the road out of our personal captivity we'll often experience raging waters, life-threatening circumstances, and violence similar to what the Israelites could see happening around them. But we, too, will come to know the continuing rescue of a supernatural God working on our behalf, and we will realize more completely the paradoxes of faith:

In powerlessness, transformation;
In surrender, a sovereign God;
In making amends for torn lives, the wholeness of God's grace;
In unexpected forgiveness, the healing of the soul;
And in shattering brokenness, a heart full of Jesus.

With our ongoing awareness of a God who leads with a cloud by day and fire by night, we feel privileged to choose, with each new day, to serve people and live rather than to use people and die.

Most of us fool ourselves. It's easy to fudge a little and feel like we're getting away with it. So we surf for porn late at night so the wife will never know. We seek the approval of others because we all need a little encouragement. We obsess about the future because we deserve a better life. We eat ice cream and Snickers because a hard life needs a little pleasure. And we refuse to forgive a friend who feels no need to change.

We seldom recognize the reality that with each act motivated by lust or anger or greed or self-interest, we sacrifice the full life of living out loud. When Jesus dwelled among us, he stated his loving intention: "I came so they can have real and eternal life, more and better life than they ever dreamed of" (John 10:10 MSG). Will we take Jesus at his word, or do we continue to carve worthless idols, each of which fails to fill our lives with purpose, value, joy, and love?

Exodus closes with this picture: "So the cloud of the LORD was over the tabernacle by day, and fire was in the cloud by night, in the sight of all the house of Israel during all their travels" (Exodus 40:38).

Imagine the glory of a supernatural God, appearing in a cloud by day and a fire by night, leading and transforming you through his power and love. By his grace, you are able to admit your own powerlessness to save yourself, and you surrender to this God of the cosmos, who just so happens to know your name and number the hair on your head.

Imagine living with the freedom to take a personal inventory of your life—safe in God's grace and safe to seek to make amends to the people you have hurt, extending to others the same kind of grace and love God and his people have extended to you.

And imagine the community of others finding a mysterious hope, power, and love along the road out to freedom. This is possible, as I and so many others have experienced. Jesus really does set people free, and he wants you to be free. So reach out to him in faith, trust him, and keep walking the path to freedom. We experience the essence of God when, through faith, we receive his grace.

Marked for Life

A short time after he takes his first steps with the help of parallel bars, Sherman walks into the tattoo shop and explains to the artist what he desires.

As the man begins his work, Sherman barely notices the pain, overshadowed as it is by his enthusiasm to share the reasons for the tattoos he has chosen. As he once again lists the miracles in his life, Sherman realizes it's not so much his story he is sharing, but God's.

Sherman's story of addiction would have ended in death or paralysis of soul, except that God's story yields redemption, value, and purpose. Sherman's story was about isolation and alienation; God's story includes a cast, a community, of friends like Mark. Sherman's story was headed toward the dead end of self-seeking; God's story brings new life, his active and animating Spirit meeting Sherman precisely at the points of his own helplessness, dependence, surrender, and desire to make amends and serve others.

When the artist says he is finished, he and Sherman examine the tattoos together—two words, one on the back of his left arm, the other on the back of his right.

Truly Blessed *is what Sherman lives to say.*

Just a Minute

Look again at the recap of Sherman's life—and then look back at your own life. Identify points where God intervened and what he graciously and lovingly added to your life. For what specific reasons do you consider yourself "Truly Blessed"?

Acknowledgments

A special word of thanks to:

The amazing people who allowed their stories to be shared in *Hope on the Broken Road*. Even though your names and situations were changed, your courage to share your life and allow all of us to learn from you is remarkable. Thanks for your transparency and for being willing to go back and revisit some old wounds for the sake of others.

The people and staff of Central Christian Church, who allow me to be myself and who are gracious enough to overlook my faults. I love serving alongside you.

The people of Hillside Christian Church, who loved me when I was a mess and who were a community for me as I walked my broken road to freedom.

The *Hope on the Broken Road* team: Chris Ferebee, Rob

Birkhead, Rob Wilkins, and Bob Wood. You are an amazing group of people to work with. Each of you in your own way made this a much better book.

Lori, the love of my life; the glue that holds our family together; the calming presence no matter how busy life gets.

Emma and Ethan, who bring me so much love and who teach me about God every day. May your lives be characterized by God's freedom.

Jesus, for the best twenty-two years of my life. I am forever grateful.

Notes

CHAPTER 2

1. The names and details shared in the stories throughout this book have been changed to protect people's privacy. All stories are used by permission.

CHAPTER 4

1. Eugene Peterson, *Christ Plays in Ten Thousand Places* (Grand Rapids, MI: Eerdmans, 2005), 164–65.

CHAPTER 5

1. Henri Nouwen, *Life of the Beloved* (New York: Crossroads, 1992), 21.

CHAPTER 10

1. Tim Keller, *Counterfeit Gods: The Empty Promises of Money, Sex, and Power, and the Only Hope That Matters* (New York: Dutton, 2009), 172.

CHAPTER 11

1. Philip Graham Ryken, *Exodus: Saved for God's Glory* (Wheaton, IL: Crossway, 2005), 1160.
2. Brennan Manning, *The Ragamuffin Gospel* (Sisters, OR: Multnomah, 2005), 31–32.

About the Author

Jud Wilhite serves as senior pastor of Central Christian Church. More than 17,000 attend Central's campuses each weekend. Jud is the author of several books, including *Eyes Wide Open: See and Live the Real You* and *Uncensored Grace: Stories of Hope from the Streets of Vegas.* Jud and his wife, Lori, reside in the Las Vegas area with their two children and a slobbery bulldog named Roxy.

WORTHY

P U B L I S H I N G

If you enjoyed this book, will you consider
sharing the message with others?

- Mention the book in a Facebook post, Twitter update,
  Pinterest pin, or blog post.
- Recommend this book to those in your small group, book
  club, workplace, and classes.
- Head over to facebook.com/judwilhite, "LIKE" the
  page, and post a comment as to what you enjoyed the most.
- Tweet "I recommend reading #HopeontheBrokenRoad by @
  judwilhite // @worthypub"
- Pick up a copy for someone you know who would be
  challenged and encouraged by this message.
- Write a book review online.

**You can subscribe to Worthy Publishing's newsletter
at www.worthypublishing.com**

**WORTHY PUBLISHING
FACEBOOK PAGE**

**WORTHY PUBLISHING
WEBSITE**